w Others

revealing look in
r nations view A
many American
ling. What man
ted may not be
always reflect
to see. Lloyd
ership and pe
Americas and
rican compl
Americans
le of the Un
ope have th
stern Europe
their collec
those of th
he people
rld's peace
the Soviet
se leadersh
come to t
aten.
This

D1495234

How Others See Us

is Volume III of a series of fourteen to be published for the Commission on Critical Choices for Americans. (See back of jacket for other titles.) The Commission is a group of 42 citizens brought together by Nelson A. Rockefeller to develop information and insights which would bring about a greater understanding of the problems confronting America. The Commission identifies the critical choices that must be made if these problems are to be met. The volumes represent the work of more than 120 distinguished authorities in such areas as energy, environment and economics; food, health and population; raw materials; national defense and international relations, and the quality of life.

Lloyd A. Free is president of the Institute for International Social Research, which to date has polled one-third of the world's population. Earlier, he was a lecturer at Princeton University, associate director of the Princeton Public Opinion Project and editor of "Public Opinion Quarterly." Subsequently, he served as senior counsellor in charge of mass communications at UNESCO and later directed the Department of State's worldwide information program. He has been an advisor to Presidents Eisenhower, Kennedy and Johnson.

How Others See Us

How Others
See Us

Critical Choices
for Americans

Volume III

Lloyd A. Free

Lexington Books
D.C. Heath and Company
Lexington, Massachusetts
Toronto   London

Library of Congress Cataloging in Publication Data

Free, Lloyd A.
    How others see us.

    (Critical choices for Americans; v.3)
    Includes index.
    1. United States—Foreign opinion. I. Commission on Critical Choices
for Americans. II. Title. III. Series.
E744.5.F73   301.15'43'973   75-44720
ISBN 0-669-00420-0

Published simultaneously in Canada.

Printed in the United States of America.

International Standard Book Number: 0-669-00420-0

Library of Congress Catalog Card Number: 75-44720

Foreword

The Commission on Critical Choices for Americans, a nationally representative, bipartisan group of forty-two prominent Americans, was brought together on a voluntary basis by Nelson A. Rockefeller. After assuming the Vice Presidency of the United States, Mr. Rockefeller, the chairman of the Commission, became an ex officio member. The Commission's assignment was to develop information and insights which would bring about a better understanding of the problems confronting America. The Commission sought to identify the critical choices that must be made if these problems are to be met.

The Commission on Critical Choices grew out of a New York State study of the Role of a Modern State in a Changing World. This was initiated by Mr. Rockefeller, who was then Governor of New York, to review the major changes taking place in federal-state relationships. It became evident, however, that the problems confronting New York State went beyond state boundaries and had national and international implications.

In bringing the Commission on Critical Choices together, Mr. Rockefeller said:

As we approach the 200th Anniversary of the founding of our Nation, it has become clear that institutions and values which have accounted for our astounding progress during the past two centuries are straining to cope with the massive problems of the current era. The increase in the tempo of change, and the vastness and complexity of the wholly new situations which are evolving with accelerated change, create a widespread sense that our political and social system has serious inadequacies.

We can no longer continue to operate on the basis of reacting to crises, counting on crash programs and the expenditure of huge sums of money to solve our problems. We have got to understand and project present trends, to take command of the forces that are emerging, to extend our freedom and wellbeing as citizens and the future of other nations and peoples in the world.

Because of the complexity and interdependence of issues facing America and the world today, the Commission has organized its work into six panels, which emphasize the interrelationships of critical choices rather than treating each one in isolation.

The six panels are:

Panel I: Energy and its Relationship to Ecology, Economics and World Stability;

Panel II: Food, Health, World Population and Quality of Life;

Panel III: Raw Materials, Industrial Development, Capital Formation, Employment and World Trade;

Panel IV: International Trade and Monetary Systems, Inflation and the Relationships Among Differing Economic Systems;

Panel V: Change, National Security and Peace

Panel VI: Quality of Life of Individuals and Communities in the U.S.A.

The Commission assigned, in these areas, more than 100 authorities to prepare expert studies in their fields of special competence. The Commission's work has been financed by The Third Century Corporation, a New York not-for-profit organization. The corporation has received contributions from individuals and foundations to advance the Commission's activities.

The Commission is determined to make available to the public these background studies and the reports of those panels which have completed their deliberations. The background studies are the work of the authors and do not necessarily represent the views of the Commission or its members.

This volume is one of the series of volumes the Commission will publish in the belief that it will contribute to the basic thought and foresight America will need in the future.

WILLIAM J. RONAN
Acting Chairman
Commission on Critical Choices
for Americans

Members of the Commission

THE HONORABLE JOHN RHODES
  Minority Leader
  United States House of Representatives

Acting Chairman

WILLIAM J. RONAN
  Chairman, Port Authority of New York
  and New Jersey

Members

IVAN ALLAN, JR.
  Former Mayor of Atlanta, Georgia

MARTIN ANDERSON
  Senior Fellow, Hoover Institution of War,
  Revolution and Peace, Stanford University

ROBERT O. ANDERSON
  Chairman, Atlantic Richfield Company

MRS. W. VINCENT ASTOR
  Philanthropist and Author

WILLIAM O. BAKER
  President, Bell Telephone Laboratories, Inc.

DANIEL J. BOORSTIN
  Senior Historian, Smithsonian Institution

NORMAN ERNEST BORLAUG
  Agronomist; Nobel Peace Prize, 1970

ERNEST L. BOYER
  Chancellor, State University of New York

GUIDO CALABRESI
  John Thomas Smith Professor of Law,
  Yale University

CLARE BOOTHE LUCE
Author; former Ambassador
and Member of Congress

PAUL WINSTON McCRACKEN
Professor of Business Administration,
University of Michigan

DANIEL PATRICK MOYNIHAN
The United States Representative to
the United Nations

BESS MYERSON
Former Commissioner of Consumer Affairs,
City of New York

WILLIAM S. PALEY
Chairman of the Board
Columbia Broadcasting System

RUSSELL W. PETERSON
Chairman, Council on Environmental
Quality

WILSON RILES
Superintendent of Public Instruction,
State of California

LAURANCE S. ROCKEFELLER
Environmentalist and Businessman

OSCAR M. RUEBHAUSEN
Partner, Debevoise, Plimpton, Lyons
and Gates, New York

GEORGE P. SHULTZ
Executive Vice President
Bechtel Corporation

JOSEPH C. SWIDLER
Partner, Leva, Hawes, Symington, Martin
& Oppenheimer
Former Chairman, Federal Power Commission

EDWARD TELLER
  Senior Research Fellow, Hoover Institution
  on War, Revolution and Peace,
  Stanford University

ARTHUR K. WATSON*
  Former Ambassador to France

MARINA VON NEUMANN WHITMAN
  Distinguished Public Service Professor
  of Economics, University of Pittsburgh

CARROLL L. WILSON
  Professor, Alfred P. Sloan
  School of Management,
  Massachusetts Institute of Technology

GEORGE D. WOODS
  Former President, World Bank

Members of the Commission served on the panels. In addition, others assisted
the panels.

BERNARD BERELSON
Senior Fellow
President Emeritus
The Population Council

C. FRED BERGSTEN
Senior Fellow
The Brookings Institution

ORVILLE G. BRIM, JR.
President
Foundation for Child Development

LESTER BROWN
President
Worldwatch Institute

LLOYD A. FREE
President
Institute for International Social Research

*Deceased

J. GEORGE HARRAR
Former President
Rockefeller Foundation

WALTER LEVY
Economic Consultant

PETER G. PETERSON
Chairman of the Board
Lehman Brothers

ELSPETH ROSTOW
Dean, Division of General and Comparative Studies
University of Texas

WALTER W. ROSTOW
Professor of Economics and History
University of Texas

SYLVESTER L. WEAVER
Communications Consultant

JOHN G. WINGER
Vice President
Energy Economics Division
Chase Manhattan Bank

Preface

The American people do not often have an opportunity to learn how the people of other countries view us, our country and our leadership role in the world. All too often, we must go only by what we read in the newspapers and watch on television, and we have little opportunity, except in travel, to understand other people's basic attitudes towards us and towards their own future.

The Commission on Critical Choices for Americans felt it important that, in an increasingly interdependent world, Americans, in making their choices, should have a better knowledge of how others view this country and Americans themselves. To do so, the Commission asked Dr. Lloyd A. Free and the Institute for International Research to interview the people and the leadership in Western Europe, the Americas and Japan.

For many Americans, the results of the survey will be surprising. What many of us have always taken for granted may not be true. The mirror does not always reflect the image we would like to see. But from it, we can, as a people, gain a greater understanding of the concerns that motivate other people and other nations in a world where the problems of one nation are often the problems of all nations. We should try to bear this in mind when we make our choices for the future.

W.J.R.

Contents

List of Tables

Introduction

The United States is not popular abroad these days, perhaps understandably, but Americans may be surprised to learn that the people of America's closest friends and major allies consider the basic interests of America and their own countries only fairly well in agreement, if at all. Yet, these same people see the United States as the world's peacemaker.

This survey of elite and popular opinion in Western Europe, the Americas, and Japan was undertaken by the Institute for International Social Research on behalf of the Commission on Critical Choices for Americans. From it, the American people can learn of the current views and concerns of the people in the nations with which this country is most closely identified; not the actions and activities of these people as portrayed through newspaper headlines and foreign policy statements, but their everyday viewpoints, attitudes, and concerns about America and themselves.

While Americans rarely question that the interests of the United States and Western Europe are fundamentally oriented toward the same goals, Western Europeans are not at all convinced this is so. In fact, their collective interests no longer fit neatly with those of the United States. The Western Europeans see their future with their neighbor countries in the European Economic Community and subordinate the United States. Similarly, Mexico and Brazil opt for their neighbors in the growth of Latin America.

The principal hold out, surprisingly, is the British public, which prefers close ties with America over close ties with Western Europe. The British intellectual elite opts for the European Economic Community. This difference of impression about America is reminiscent, in a sense, of the division of opinion in Britain during the Civil War in this country. Had it been left to the British elite, Britain's support would have gone to the Confederacy. Yet, they were unable to commit their country to the South because of the overwhelming support of the British public for the Union.

As for Japan, its amazing people seem to forget more and more each day that they are geographically part of Asia. The Japanese responded to most of the questions in the survey just like Western Europeans. They identify with Americans and Western Europeans. They desire improved relations with China but express no interest in Southeast Asia and the rest of their one-time co-prosperity sphere.

The United States is, however, regarded by its neighbors as the most capable and the most appropriate nation to provide leadership in striving for world peace. The so-called fear of the United States as an imperial power did not show up in this survey. The United States, furthermore, ranked well ahead of the Soviet Union in its capacity for wise leadership in international affairs. Although, the fear of war is at its lowest in over twenty years, most people surveyed believe, ironically, that the United States will spare nothing in coming to their defense. This, despite the current talk of an American return to isolationism, even in France which has mostly withdrawn from NATO.

Similarly, the people interviewed reject the notion of five superpowers in the years ahead—a pentagonal structure of the United States, the Soviet Union, China, Japan, and the Common Market countries. They continue to see only two superpowers, the United States and the Soviet Union, in roughly equal strength. This illustrates that the French have not taken to heart the illusion of grandeur fostered by their late leader. Also, two countries with very great potential for a larger world role, Japan and Germany, show almost no interest in achieving it.

Only Brazil among the countries surveyed sees itself as a great nation in the future—a view wholeheartedly supported not only by the leadership but by the entire populace. The saying, "Have no fear. God is a Brazilian and He will take care of Brazil," appears to have been taken literally to heart by the people of this rapidly growing new giant in the world.

In every country two samples, each consisting of approximately six hundred cases, were interviewed: namely, national cross-sections of the general public and of the socioeconomic elite. The nations involved, and in parentheses the names of the local research organizations that did the interviewing, coding, and tabulating for us under subcontract, are as follows:

> Great Britain (Research Services)
> France (Cofremca)
> West Germany (Emnid-Institut)
> Italy (Doxa)
> Japan (Shin Joho Center)
> Canada (Market Facts)
> Mexico (International Research Associates)
> Brazil (Instituto Gallup de Opiniao Publica)

The interviewing was conducted more or less simultaneously in the countries involved, for the most part during the period from late October to mid-December, 1974. The questions were designed to focus on issues of "timeless" concern. The objective was to get at the realities that are not immediately subject to instant crises and to reach the cares that endure.

The cross-sections of the various publics were based on what technically are called random samples of the population eighteen years of age or over. In Mexico and Brazil, because earlier surveys had shown us that the rural people know so little about public affairs that it is useless to interview them about international matters, the samples were confined to people living in cities of 50,000 or more. In all other countries, however, cross-sections included all elements of the population, urban and rural.

The samples of the elites were confined to the top 10 percent (in fact, in most cases 6 or 7 percent) of the socioeconomic pyramid in each country. The interviewing was conducted in affluent sections of cities with populations of 100,000 or more and respondents had to be at least thirty years of age. They qualified either through the fact that (1) they had at least some university education themselves; or (2) that they or their husbands were in the top income, social class, or occupational categories.

Detailed explanations of the system of Composite Scores used extensively throughout this report and of the method of computing ladder ratings, which appear in two chapters, can be found in the appendixes of *State of the Nation 1974*, by William Watts and the present author, published by Potomac Associates in 1974.

Along with the subcontractors who did the interviewing, my gratitude goes to Dr. Albert H. Cantril and Charles W. Roll, Jr., who served as consultants in helping devise the original questionnaire, and particularly to our assistant secretary-treasurer, Miss Kathryn A. Hathaway, who made many of the necessary computations and was responsible for reproducing the manuscript.

In sum, this study was undertaken by the Commission on Critical Choices in order to give the American people a much more realistic picture of how others really view America, Americans and their own countries. As Robert Burns said, *"Oh wad some power the giftie gie us, to see oursels as others see us!"* This study provides such an opportunity.

LLOYD A. FREE
President
Institute for International
Social Research

I International Cooperation and Orientations

Every individual has his own "reality world"—that is, the particular ways in which he perceives the realities of the world in which he lives and the significances he reads into what he sees as realities. While many aspects of each person's reality world are unique, there are also many sectors more or less common within a particular culture or cultures. Depending upon the subject matter, intercultural variations are often distinct, significant, and of actual or potential import in affecting not only attitudes, but behavior, whether individual or mass.

Particularly in the field of international affairs, there are enormous variations; among other things, in the awareness, knowledge, and horizons that different individuals, groups, and peoples bring to bear in viewing the globe; and, connectedly, in their orientations having to do with international relationships.

To obtain an overview of the outlooks of publics and elites in the eight countries surveyed in three very different parts of the world, we first probed to get at the countries, regions, and international bodies which loomed sufficiently important in their minds to be mentioned voluntarily by our respondents. Obviously, ideas about international cooperation are indicative of international orientations in one of the broadest and most meaningful of senses. Without any probing or reminders, they were asked the following question:

QUESTION: *To start with, I would like to ask you a question or two about international cooperation. First, with which countries do you think (respondent's country) should cooperate* very closely *under present circumstances? And with which international organizations should we cooperate* very closely?

1

The Canadians

The countries and organizations which at least 10 percent of one or the other samples of our Canadian neighbors thought their own nation should cooperate with very closely are listed in Table I-1.

Casting these results into still broader areas by combining some of the items listed, we come out with these major focuses of Canadian international orientations:

	Elite	Public
The United Nations and its specialized agencies	75%	45%
Western European countries or organizations	90	67
The United States	73	71
The Atlantic Alliance	32	24
Asian countries or organizations	51	36
The USSR and other Eastern European countries	36	32
Arab, Middle East, or African countries	21	11
Latin American countries or organizations	19	6
International relief or charitable organizations	19	14
Commonwealth countries (particularly Australia and New Zealand)	10	8

This listing demonstrates that, when it comes to ideas about international cooperation, the Canadians undoubtedly have horizons of broader scope not only than those of any of other samples we surveyed, but, on the basis of our studies, of any other people in the world with the possible exception of the Americans. While rooted, apart from the United Nations, primarily in Western Europe and the United States, with the Atlantic Alliance serving as a bridge to both, their orientations extended in very significant degree to Eastern Europe, the Middle East, Africa, Latin America, and Asia as well.

Also, relatively few Canadians were unable or unwilling to mention any country with which Canada should cooperate (9 percent of the public; only 2 percent of the elite) or any organization (38 percent of the public; 11 percent of the elite). In short the international orientations of Canadians tend to be both truly outgoing and worldwide.

The Japanese

In sharp contrast to the Canadians, what the Japanese have in the forefront of their minds when asked about international orientations is much more severely restricted. Table I-2 summarizes responses, amounting to 5 percent or more of at suggestions at all. Assumedly one reason for this is that the Japanese are both sensitive and ambivalent about pushing to establish closer relations in their own part of the world in view of the evidences of anti-Japanese feeling, vestigial to their role in World War II, which have erupted from time to time in various parts of Asia. Indicative of this, along with the very large proportions who refused to name any specific country at all, are the fairly large percentages who gave the highly ambiguous reply of "all countries."

A second possible thread to their thinking in this regard is suggested by the results on the following question which was asked after the ones just discussed:

QUESTION: *More generally, would you favor or oppose Japan and other non-Communist countries of Asia grouping together more closely to provide more of a counterbalance to mainland China?*

	Elite	Public
Favor	38%	24%
Oppose	29	29
Don't know	33	47
	100%	100%

Both the very large percentages replying "don't know" and the considerable proportions "opposed" indicate very considerable hesitancy about giving the Chinese, with whom the Japanese definitely want closer relationships, any impression that the Japanese are anti-Chinese. It is quite possible that a good many Japanese feel that for their country to establish closer relations in other parts of Asia would be viewed as a potentially hostile or damaging move by the mainland Chinese.

The Mexicans and Brazilians

Unlike the Japanese, among whom, apart from mainland China, mentions of countries or organizations in their own region (Asia) were sparse, the primary focus of the Mexicans and Brazilians, along with the United Nations, was on Latin America. Combining the figures for each of the two samples in both countries and dividing by two to give averages, we come out with Table I-3, which includes mentions of at least 5 percent of those countries and organizations with which they felt their own countries should cooperate very closely.

Obviously, references to other countries in Latin America were far more frequent than to the United States. And, most indicatively, the combined Mexican and Brazilian elites referred to cooperation with Western European

Table I-3
International Cooperation: Countries, Regions Preferred by Mexicans and Brazilians

	Elites	Publics
The United Nations and its specialized agencies	68%	42%
Latin American countries	57	43
Western European countries and organizations	32	23
The Organization of American States and other organizations of the Americas	34	17
The United States	28	37
African or Middle Eastern countries	12	9
Japan	11	9
China	5	5
Other Asian countries	8	5
The Soviet Union	6	6

countries or organizations with higher frequency than with the United States. Significant attention, although in lesser degree than among the Canadians, was also given to Africa, the Middle East, and Asia.

While the "don't know" percentages among the elites were relatively small, 16 percent of the Mexican and Brazilian publics did not mention any country at all with which their own should cooperate, and more than one-half made the same omission in the case of international organizations. Thus, like the Japanese at the public level the international horizons of our Latin American neighbors tend to be somewhat restricted; but, unlike the Japanese, the predominant focus, apart from the United Nations, is on their own part of the world.

In fact, when asked specifically about this matter, the proportions saying they would like to see relations between their own country and some of the other nations in Latin America become closer reached 64 percent in the case of the Mexican public, 70 percent among the Brazilian elite, and 75 percent among the Mexican elite. The reactions of the Brazilian public were not quite the same: 48 percent wanted closer relations, but an almost equal 44 percent said they were satisfied with the present situation (the remaining 8 percent gave "don't know" answers).

Those who said they wanted closer relations in general were pinned down as to the specific countries they had in mind. The specific countries mentioned by at least 10 percent of the public or elite samples are listed in Table I-4.

It is interesting to note that, while the Mexican samples referred to cooperation with Brazil with higher frequency than any other country, the Brazilian samples mentioned Mexico with a frequency of only 7 percent in the case of the elite and 5 percent among the public. Another factor of note is that

Table I-4
International Cooperation: Preferences of Latin American Countries

	Mexicans			Brazilians	
	Elite	Public		Elite	Public
Brazil	40%	30%	Argentina	34%	21%
Argentina	38	25	Bolivia	12	9
Venezuela	28	17	Uruguay	17	10
Chile	17	15	Chile	13	6
Peru	15	12	Venezuela	15	9
Guatemala	12	9	Paraguay	13	8
			Peru	10	6
			All Latin American countries	19	12

Cuba received attention from only 7 percent of both the public and elite samples in Mexico and only 3 percent of the Brazilian elite and 2 percent of the public.

The Western Europeans

The same concentration close to home evident among the Latin Americans also pertained in the four Western European countries surveyed. To simplify our presentation, we shall first list the averages amounting to at least 5 percent that emerged from our samples of Western Europeans as a whole, then comment both on less mentioned countries and organizations, and on variations among the four countries involved. The overall figures in Table I-5 were calculated by taking total mentions across-the-board and then dividing by the number of pertinent countries.

Putting together some of the totals, it becomes clear that the chief priorities in regard to international cooperation in the minds of Western Europeans were: (1) first and foremost, the European Economic Community and countries in Western Europe; (2) the United States and the Atlantic Alliance; (3) the United Nations and its specialized agencies; and (4) the Soviet Union and Eastern Europe. Rated significantly lower were (5) the main sources of imported oil; and (6) interregional monetary and trade bodies, on the one hand, and international relief and charitable organizations, on the other. In view of Western European dependence on oil imports, it is worthy of note that references to the oil producing countries in general and the Arab and Middle Eastern nations in particular were surprisingly low.

Although not shown in Table I-5, the detailed figures reveal that, apart from British references to Canada, mentions of any countries in the Western

Table I-5

International Cooperation: Countries, Regions Preferred by Western Europeans

	Elites	Publics
The European Economic Community (or Common Market)	56%	33%
Specified Western European countries or Western Europe in general	20	16
The United Nations and its specialized agencies	54	30
The United States	41	38
The Atlantic Alliance	26	16
The Soviet Union	10	11
Other Eastern European countries or Eastern Europe in general	18	13
Oil-producing countries, particularly the Arab or Middle East nations	9	7
Interregional monetary and trade organizations	6	2
International relief and charitable organizations	5	5

Hemisphere other than the United States were at very low ebb, as were references to any of the African countries apart from the Arab or Middle Eastern nations. Somewhat surprisingly, only 3 percent of the public samples across-the-board and 4 percent of the elite called to mind mainland China and 2 percent of each Japan.

As would be expected, references to the Commonwealth countries in general and to Canada, Australia, and New Zealand in particular were high among the British. In contrast, very few of our French respondents (2 percent of the public, 4 percent of the elite) mentioned the former French colonies. While the British still seem to cling to current ties with their old Empire, the French as a matter of present-day realities appear not to.

As evidence of the limited horizons of many of our respondents, 16 percent of the public samples as a whole could not, or did not mention any country at all with which their own should cooperate closely, while the corresponding figure with respect to international organizations zoomed to 42 percent. In short, a surprising proportion of Western Europeans, appear to be internation-ally-minded only on a rather narrow canvas, if at all.

In a number of cases, frequency of mentions varied considerably in respects other than those mentioned above among the people in the four Western European countries surveyed. Fluctuations were especially interesting, for example, in mentions of each other, the European Common Market, and various other countries in Western Europe. These are shown in Table I-6. *The reason some of the totals exceed 100 percent is that multiple mentions were involved.*

It will be seen from the totals in Table I-6 that the Germans had by far the strongest orientation toward Western Europe, followed rather far behind by the

Table I-6
International Cooperation: Preferences Within Western Europe

References to:	Elites				Publics			
	British	French	German	Italians	British	French	German	Italians
EEC	57%	41%	70%	57%	25%	25%	50%	33%
Britain	*	8	16	9	*	7	15	5
France	17	*	31	15	15	*	33	10
Germany	19	23	*	26	18	22	*	20
Italy	5	3	3	*	2	3	4	*
Scandinavian or Benelux	12	6	6	4	12	4	5	3
Other Western European countries	3	2	5	5	*	1	9	5
	113%	83%	131%	116%	72%	62%	116%	76%

Italians. Perhaps the most illuminating aspect of the findings has to do with an almost incredible shift in British orientations. From the outlook of a world power which for years scorned affiliation with Europe, they have become almost equally oriented toward cooperation with Western Europe as the Italians. Also surprising, perhaps, is that the French proved to be the least interested of all in cooperation with the EEC and other countries within Western Europe. However, perhaps too sweepingly, the French always have been more interested in leading Western Europe than in cooperating with its various components.

Going into more detail, it will be seen that the Italians referred to close cooperation with Germany will almost double the frequency as compared to France and treble or more as to Britain. Both the samples in Germany spoke of France with much greater frequency than of either Britain or Italy. Conversely, French references to Germany were far ahead of those either to Britain or Italy. In the eyes of the Germans and the French, it would appear, the relationship between their own two nations constitutes the very heart of Western Europe.

In contrast, both the public and elite samples in Britain referred to close cooperation with the Scandanavian or Benelux countries with a frequency of 12 percent, far higher than in any of the other countries surveyed, while their mentions of France, although more frequent, were still only in the 15 percent to 17 percent range, and of Germany, 18 percent to 19 percent. Quite clearly, the Europe of the British tends to be somewhat more broadly based than that of the French, Germans, or Italians.

The most interesting variations from the American point of view were, of course, in the number of references to the United States itself and to the

Atlantic Alliance, which are listed in Table I-7 with the Canadian figures added for purposes of comparison.

Thus the leaders by far in mentioning close cooperation with the United States and NATO were the Canadians. They were followed among the Western Europeans by the Germans and in third place by the British. Considerably back of them came the Italians and then the French.

For purposes of comparison we shall add parenthetically at this point the percentages of mentions of the United States, as such, in the three other countries surveyed, where references to the Atlantic Alliance were not in order because they were not members:

	References to the United States	
	Elites	Publics
Japanese	55%	37%
Mexican	32	49
Brazilian	24	24

The rough impressions to be derived from these figures (although direct comparisons with the earlier ones on the NATO countries are not entirely feasible) are that in a very general way the Japanese and Mexicans are in somewhat the same league as the Italians, while the Brazilians are more similar to the French in relatively low concern about close cooperation with America.

Table I-7
International Cooperation: Preferences for the United States and NATO

	References to:		
	The United States	The Atlantic Alliance	Combined Total
Elites			
Canadian	73%	32%	105%
German	52	36	88
British	47	37	84
Italian	38	15	53
French	27	17	44
Publics			
Canadian	71	24	95
German	53	29	82
British	39	17	56
Italian	39	9	48
French	22	7	29

Preference for Closer Ties with Europe than with the United States

Despite the relatively large number of references to the United States and the Atlantic Alliance, the predominant orientations of Western Europeans tended to be focused on their own region. This fact was strongly underlined by the results from the following question asked later in the interviews:

> QUESTION: *If you had to choose between closer ties with other Western European nations or closer ties with the United States, which would you choose: other European nations or the United States?*

The results are given in Table I-8.

Thus, large majorities of both the elite and public samples in France and Germany would choose the Western European nations over the United States, plus majorities of the Italian and British elites and a plurality of the Italian public. The hold-out in this respect turned out to be the British public.

Undoubtedly the most significant of these results is the fact that, in the face of earlier ideas about their special relationship with America, the British elite overwhelmingly endorsed preference for Europe over the United States and the Atlantic Alliance.

Also surprising to one who has followed opinion currents in these countries over many years are the results among Italians. They had tended to cling stubbornly, and on occasion even somewhat desperately to their bond with America during the earlier postwar period. However, by now, their primary focus is also on Western Europe.

Table I-8
Preferences Between Ties with Europe and the United States

		Would Choose:		
		European Nations	United States	Don't Know
Elites				
	French	79%	12%	9%
	German	68	23	9
	Italian	73	22	5
	British	71	23	6
Publics				
	French	64	15	21
	German	63	22	15
	Italian	47	33	20
	British	42	50	8

II The European Economic Community

One of the reasons why closer ties with Western Europe loom larger in the minds of the Europeans than ties with the United States is undoubtedly that the Europeans do not feel that the basic interests of America and their own interests as a collectivity are to any marked extent in agreement.

Mutuality of Interests Between the Common Market and the United States

This became clear when our Western European samples were asked the following two questions:

> QUESTIONS: 1. *Under present circumstances, do you think in general that the basic political interests of the United States and those of the Common Market countries as a whole are very much in agreement, fairly well in agreement, rather different, or very different?*
> 2. *And do you think the basic economic interests of the United States and those of the Common Market countries as a whole are very much in agreement, fairly well in agreement, rather different, or very different?*

To facilitate comparative analysis where so many different statistics are involved, we will resort in much of this report to a system of composite scoring yielding one overall figure which demonstrates the general thrust of all the answers to a particular query. Thus on the questions above, the answer "very much in agreement" has been scored at 100 points; "fairly well in agreement" at two-thirds of 100; "rather different" at one-third of 100; "very different" at zero. Obviously under this system the median point between positive and negative replies is 50. In this particular case, any composite score above this indicates a preponderance of opinion towards the "fairly well in agreement" side; any score below 50, a predominance toward the "rather different" view.

To illustrate this technique we shall now give the detailed results from two of the samples included in our surveys and below these the composite scores that resulted.

	Elites	
	German	French
Interests of the U.S. and the Common Market Are:		
Very much in agreement	9%	5%
Fairly well in agreement	48	30
Rather different	35	44
Very different	6	16
Don't know	2	5
	100%	100%
Composite Scores	54	42

The positive score (meaning above 50) among the German elite indicated a prevailing view (although not very pronounced) that the basic interests of the Common Market countries and America were at least somewhat in agreement. The negative score (below 50) in the case of the French elite definitely indicated they thought otherwise.

Utilizing this technique on the results from all the samples to the two questions quoted above, we come out with the composite scores listed in Table II-1. The so-called combined averages in the right-hand column were obtained by adding the ratings from the elite and the public samples in each country and dividing by two; the overall averages at the bottom by adding all the scores in each column and dividing by four.

Thus, in terms of congruence of both political and economic interests, the across-the-board overall averages were relatively low: 52 and 51. Since these hover near the median point of 50, they indicate that there was no preponderance of opinion among Western Europeans as a whole either toward the favorable or the unfavorable sides—in short, a virtual standoff. In large part this was due to the fairly negative scores turned in by both French samples. It is clear

Table II-1
Mutuality of Interests: United States and Common Market
(Composite Scores)

	Elites	Publics	Combined Averages
Mutuality of Political Interests			
British	54	50	52
French	45	40	43
Germans	57	54	56
Italians	57	58	58
Overall Averages	53	51	52
Mutality of Economic Interests			
British	53	51	52
French	42	42	42
Germans	54	51	53
Italians	51	58	55
Overall Averages	50	51	51

that the French, both public and elite, tend to feel that the interests of the Common Market and those of the United States are at best "rather different." Offsetting the French results were the higher ratings in Germany and Italy; but even these leaned only moderately toward the "fairly well in agreement" side.

In short, the Western Europeans are not at all convinced that their collective interests and those of the United States fit together neatly under present circumstances.

Closer Relations Between the EEC and the United States

Nevertheless, except in France, there was considerable feeling that relationships should be closer.

> QUESTION: *Do you feel that relations between the United States and the Common Market countries as a whole at present are too close, not close enough, or about right?*

The results are given in Table II-2.

It can be seen that majorities of both the British public and elite and pluralities of both the Italian samples felt relations with the United States are "not close enough." Both the German public and elite were almost evenly

Table II-2
Closeness of Relations between EEC and United States

	Elites				Publics			
	British	French	German	Italian	British	French	German	Italian
Too close	1%	27%	7%	22%	3%	16%	5%	10%
Not close enough	62	28	45	40	51	26	42	34
About right	32	35	43	31	29	33	41	29
Don't know	5	10	5	7	17	25	12	27

divided between "not close enough" and "about right." At the same time, it should be noted that 22 percent of the Italian elite and no less than 27 percent of the French elite felt that the relationship with the United States is already "too close." Nevertheless, if we average the figures across-the-board, predominant sentiment in plurality proportions favored more intimate ties between the Common Market and America.

Future Relations Between the EEC
and the United States

Looking to the future, on an overall basis there was a slightly predominant feeling that relations with the United States will stay about the same, with substantial proportions, however, predicting that they will become closer.

QUESTION: *Is it your guess that over the next five years relations between the United States and the Common Market countries as a whole will become closer, less close, or stay about the same as now?*

	Elites				Publics			
	British	French	German	Italian	British	French	German	Italian
Closer	37%	29%	27%	31%	39%	27%	24%	30%
Less close	17	14	18	20	10	12	14	10
About the same	39	41	48	35	36	30	47	30
Don't know	7	16	7	14	15	31	15	30

In other words, the French in effect thought that they would get in the future what they wanted; namely, that relations with the United States would remain as they are now. On the other hand, in the case of all the other samples, the proportions who believed relations between the Common Market and the United States would actually become closer in the future were significantly lower in each case than the percentages who, on the preceding question, wanted them to become closer. In short, a good many of our British, German, and Italian respondents anticipated that their wishes would be frustrated in this regard as the future unfolded.

Mutuality of Interests between the EEC and Japan

Similar questions about Japan and the Common Market were posed only to the elite samples.

> QUESTION: *Turning now to Japan, under present circumstances do you feel that in general the basic interests of the Common Market countries and those of Japan are very much in agreement, fairly well in agreement, rather different, or very different?*

The composite scores that emerged on this question were as follows:

Elites	
British	36
French	43
German	49
Italian	44
Overall Average	43

Although the German elite's rating was very close to the 50 mark, the overall average of 43 indicated that across-the-board opinion about the common interests of the European Economic Community and Japan was to the effect that they were not in agreement, but at least somewhat different.

The Japanese elite tended to agree with this assessment. The composite score was also below the median point of 50 (47), indicating that they too did not feel any positive mutuality of interest with the European Economic Community. In view of the history of often intense commercial rivalry between Europe and Japan, these findings, both in Western Europe and Japan, can hardly be deemed surprising.

Relations between the EEC and Japan

Nevertheless, while pluralities of the European elites, except in Italy, felt that relations with Japan should stay about as they are, there was at least a mild tendency to feel that Europe and Japan should come closer together.

QUESTION: *Do you feel that relations between Japan and the Common Market countries as a whole at present are too close, not close enough, or about right?*

	Elites				
	British	French	Germans	Italians	Overall Averages
Too close	4%	9%	3%	3%	5%
Not close enough	38	25	33	39	34
About right	40	43	47	35	41
Don't know	18	23	17	23	20

These results would seem to indicate, at the very least, that there is little if any pronounced anti-Japanese sentiment among the Western Europeans, and at least substantial (although only plurality) sentiment in favor of more intimate relations.

On the other side of the equation, a large majority of the Japanese elite favored closer ties.

QUESTION: *Do you feel that relations between Japan and the Common Market countries as a whole at present are too close, not close enough, or about right?*

	Japanese Elite
Too close	1%
Not close enough	62
About right	24
Don't know	13

Looking at the results both from Western Europe and Japan, it would thus appear that, psychologically at least, the prospect of a more intimate relationship is open.

Canada and the EEC

The Canadian elite also exhibited a lively interest in the Common Market. Here are their views on the issue of congruence between Canada's basic interests and those of the members of the Common Market:

	Canadian Elite
Very much in agreement	8%
Fairly well in agreement	52
Rather different	27
Very different	6
Don't know	7

The composite score in this case was 56, leaning toward the "fairly well in agreement" viewpoint.

The Canadian elite also definitely wanted closer ties with the EEC. When asked whether Canada's relations with the Common Market countries as a whole are too close, not close enough, or about right, the responses were:

	Canadian Elite
Too close	4%
Not close enough	55
About right	30
Don't know	11

Mutual Interests of the EEC Members

Both publics and elites in the four major nations of the EEC tended to feel that, as a whole, the basic interests of the various members were in agreement, but not in any pronounced degree.

> QUESTION: *Coming closer to home, do you feel that the basic interests of the various members of the Common Market, including our own country, are very much in agreement, fairly well in agreement, rather different, or very different under present circumstances?*

The composite scores are given in Table II-3.

Thus the French, with their paternalistic feelings about the European Economic Community, were the most positive in their views, followed to a lesser extent by the Italian public and, most interestingly, the British elite. In contrast, the publics in Britain and especially Germany, and the elite in Italy turned in scores below the median point of 50, indicating slightly negative views on this issue of mutuality of common interests. The Overall Average for

Table II-3
Mutuality of Interests Among EEC Members
(Composite Scores)

	Elites	Publics	Combined Averages
British	56	48	52
French	68	64	66
German	50	46	48
Italian	49	59	54
Overall Averages	56	54	55

both types of samples was 55, leaning only modestly toward the "fairly well in agreement" point of view.

The Common Market: Beneficial or Harmful?

Nevertheless, there was a very decided feeling in all of the countries concerned (most notably including Great Britain) that participation in the Common Market would be beneficial in national terms.

> QUESTION: *Considering the record to date, is it your judgment that, on balance, participation in the Common Market will prove beneficial or harmful to your own national interests? Is it your opinion that the Common Market will prove beneficial (harmful) to your interests a great deal or only somewhat?*

The composite scoring system used here weighted "beneficial—a great deal" answers at 100; "beneficial—somewhat" at two-thirds of 100; "harmful—somewhat" at one-third; and "harmful—a great deal" at zero. Thus any rating above 50 indicated a belief that participation in the Common Market was in some degree beneficial; anything below 50 that it was to a certain extent harmful. The results so calculated are given in Table II-4.

Thus, the prevailing view throughout, especially among the elites, was that participation in the Common Market would very definitely be beneficial to all concerned. The British figures are the most striking in view of the controversy that raged for months over the United Kingdom's continued membership in the EEC. Obviously, the British elite was overwhelming on the positive side in this respect, but the results from the British public also indicated a predominant feeling that continuing participation would help their country. These

Table II-4
Beneficial or Harmful Effects of Common Market
(Composite Scores)

	Elites	Publics	Combined Averages
British	74	57	66
French	85	71	78
German	83	75	79
Italian	75	70	73
Overall Averages	79	68	74

findings clearly presaged the overwhelming endorsement of the Common Market in the British referendum.

The findings in total suggest that, despite some doubts about the degree of mutuality of interests among its members, the Common Market is currently operating in a very favorable climate of opinion, based upon hard-headed assessments of self-interest.

Increased Unity of Western Europe

In fact, so much is this the case that very large majorities of both elites and publics, *even in Great Britain*, were in favor of further steps toward integrating Western Europe.

QUESTION: *Apart from the Common Market, are you in general for or against making further efforts towards uniting Western Europe?*

	Elites				
	British	French	German	Italian	Overall Averages
For	88%	92%	94%	94%	92%
Against	10	3	2	3	4
Don't know	2	5	4	3	4
			Publics		
For	72	83	86	79	80
Against	13	5	4	8	9
Don't know	10	12	10	13	11

With an average of eight out of ten members of the publics and more than nine out of ten of the elites supporting greater unity, it would appear from the point of view of practical politics that the future of a more collectivized Western Europe looks bright, indeed, under present circumstances.

In fact, *with the exception of the British*, predominant sentiment (in most cases very heavily so) favored going the full route to true political integration. This emerged when the following query was put to those who favored further unity on the question discussed above (thus the totals below are not 100 percent but only the percentages in each country that favored further integrating steps):

QUESTION: *Would you favor or oppose (respondent's country) joining a political federation of Western Europe in which the final authority would lie with the central government rather than with the member countries?*

	British	French	German	Italian	Overall Averages
			Elites		
For	32%	59%	71%	72%	58%
Against	51	24	16	15	27
Don't know	5	9	7	7	7
	88%	92%	94%	94%	92%
			Publics		
For	23	41	63	53	45
Against	44	19	11	13	22
Don't know	5	23	12	13	13
	72%	83%	86%	79%	80%

It will be seen that only the British were opposed. The only other degree of support below average was in the case of the French public and to a far lesser extent the French elite. Our French respondents may have been reflecting in moderate degree de Gaulle's long-term opposition to any federation of Europe which would dilute the ultimate national sovereignty of the multi-state grouping that was his goal.

Nevertheless, in general, particularly if, as, and when the British newcomers become more acclimated to operating in the EEC context, the prospects in general for a truly integrated European federation might eventually become bright, indeed.

III General Attitudes Toward the United States and American Corporations

A review of high and low points on a series of five opinion questions asked periodically by the United States Information Agency in a wide range of countries reveals the following overall fluctuations in attitudes toward the United States: (1) high between 1961 and 1965; (2) very low during 1967 and 1968 (while the United States was still heavily engaged in Indochina); and (3) mixed (some items high, some low) from 1969 to 1972.[a] Our current surveys show that mixed evaluations of this country still continued to prevail at the end of 1974.

Opinions of the United States

To start with, opinions of the United States at the abstract level still could not in general be deemed favorable, and in a number of countries remained downright unfavorable. The question asked in this respect was as follows:

QUESTION: *What is your overall opinion of the United States, its policies and actions at the present time—excellent, good, only fair, or poor?*

---

[a]The authority for this information is Dr. Alvin Richman, Office of Research, USIA. I am also deeply indebted to Dr. Leo Crespi, who for many years has directed the operational aspects of USIA's research. In order to chart trends, I have often used the wording of questions devised by him and his staff, including a good many in these current surveys.

Since in this chapter we will be dealing with two samples of each of eight countries, readers would be inundated if all the results were listed in detail. For this reason, we shall first give three sets of overall figures in Table III-1: one for our four major allies in Western Europe (Britain, France, Germany and Italy); a second for our major neighbors in this hemisphere (Canada, Mexico, and Brazil); a third for Japan.

To make comparisons easier, we shall now shift the percentages given in Table III-1 into composite scores by rating "excellent" replies at 100; "good" at two thirds of 100: "only fair" at one-third" and "poor" at zero. On this basis we come out with the following groupings:

	(Composite Scores)	
	Elites	Publics
British, French, German, Italian	42	46
Canadian, Mexican, Brazilian	39	42
Japanese	41	33

All of these ratings are obviously below the median point of 50, indicating a predominance of opinion on the negative, "only fair" side. To show variations on a country-by-country basis, Table III-2 gives the composite scores derived from each individual sample in rank order of the combined scores.

For years it has been taken for granted by experts knowledgeable about foreign public opinion that overall attitudes among the "elites" were far more negative toward the United States than those of the publics. However, looking at the overall averages at the bottom of Table III-2, we find that on a combined basis there was no statistically significant difference between the socioeconomic elites as a whole and the publics as a whole in the eight countries surveyed.

Table III-1
Opinions of the United States
(By Regions)

	Elites			Publics		
	Western Europe	The Americas	Japan	Western Europe	The Americas	Japan
Excellent	4%	4%	5%	6%	6%	2%
Good	33	27	23	34	29	16
Only fair	45	46	51	39	42	44
Poor	16	20	13	12	17	20
Don't know	2	3	8	9	6	18

Table III-2
Opinions of the United States (By Countries)
(Composite Scores)

	Elites	Publics	Combined Scores
Italian	44	54	49
British	44	48	46
German	44	46	45
Brazilian	37	48	43
Mexican	41	40	41
Canadian	39	39	39
Japanese	41	33	37
French	36	36	36
Overall Averages	41	43	42

Taking the combined scores in the third column of Table III-2 (calculated simplistically by adding the ratings by the elite and by the public and then dividing by two) we note again that all of them were below 50 and hence not favorable. However, it will be seen that the least unfavorable scores were turned in by the Italians (and especially the Italian elite, whose rating was the only one on the favorable side), closely followed by the British and the Germans; the most unfavorable by the French, Japanese, and to a slightly lesser extent the Canadians.

While these results could, of course, have been worse, we cannot say that they are good. In fact, with the variations mentioned, the predominant opinions of the United States in the countries surveyed were definitely in negative balance at the time of our surveys.

Image of America

As would be expected from the unfavorable balance of opinions about the United States, the image of America was decidedly mixed. The questions involved were as follows:

QUESTIONS: *Every country has its good points and its bad points. Taking its good points first, what do you admire most about the United States, its policies and actions? And what do you dislike most about the United States, its policies and actions?*

Once again, to cut down on the figures, we have calculated overall mentions in Britain, France, Germany, and Italy as a whole (in the column labeled "Western Europe"), then for Canada, Mexico and Brazil together (under the heading "The Americas"), and finally for Japan. The results are given in Table III-3.

In addition to those listed in Table III-3, other items proved significant in the case of the Japanese. "Maintaining military bases or introducing nuclear weapons in Japan" was referred to by 8 percent of the elite and 11 percent of the public. The huge "don't know; no answer" percentages in the case not only of the Japanese public but of the elite is understandable to anyone familiar with polling in Japan; the Japanese are undoubtedly one of the most "diplomatic" of all peoples, particularly when it comes to commenting about other countries in any specific way.

If we combine the favorable and unfavorable mentions, respectively, from all the elite and all the public samples, including some miscellaneous references not mentioned in the tables, an interesting overall picture emerges in terms of total gross percentages.

	Elites			Publics		
	Internat'l	Domestic	Total	Internat'l	Domestic	Total
Favorable	322	580	902	246	441	687
Unfavorable	446	474	920	294	416	710

The first thing to be noted in the columns labeled "Total" is that the sum of all unfavorable mentions, international and domestic, exceeded the sum of all favorable mentions among both the elites and the publics as a whole, but in both cases by very slight margins. Secondly, at both the public and especially the elite levels references to international matters was on the negative side, while the margin of domestic mentions was definitely favorable.

As a result, in sum total there were far more favorable domestic references than favorable international ones. In short, whether justified or not, foreigners seem to find more to admire in the America they perceive within its own borders than they do about the role the United States plays abroad. This fact would seem to have a certain significance in terms of the goals and operations of our international information and cultural programs.

While the gross picture given above amounts to a virtual stalemate between the positive and negative aspects of the American image, thus giving no cause for euphoria, there is clear evidence that the total results are distinctly more favorable than they were in 1968 when the Institute for International Social Research polled the publics in Britain, France, Germany, Italy, and Japan using the same image questions. The comparative results in those countries at the public level as of then and now are as follows:

| | Early 1968 | | | Late 1974 | | |
	Internat'l	Domestic	Total	Internat'l	Domestic	Total
Favorable	132	136	268	168	247	415
Unfavorable	272	193	465	165	255	420

Thus the image these publics had of the United States in the seven countries listed above in 1968 was negative on the domestic side and highly so on the international (in part because of the Vietnam war). As a result, total unfavorable references then vastly exceeded favorable ones. In contrast, our current surveys show these same publics virtually evenly divided between favorable and unfavorable references in terms both of domestic and international matters and hence virtually stalemated when it came to positive and negative mentions in total.

In short, although it is still not good, the image of the United States is a lot better than it was six years ago in the sense that it has shifted from highly adverse to neutral.

Mutuality of Interests with the United States

Although the United States cannot be said to be "popular" these days, nevertheless a very reassuring sense of mutual interests between America and her major allies and neighbors still persists.

> QUESTION: *Is it your impression that in general the basic interests of (respondent's own country) and those of the United States are very much in agreement, fairly well in agreement, rather different, or very different?*

Again to reduce the flood of figures, in Table III-4 we give combined percentages for Britain, France, Germany, and Italy as a group ("Western Europe"); then for Canada, Mexico, and Brazil ("The Americas"), and finally for Japan.

It will be noted that in each case the preponderance of answers was in the "fairly well in agreement" category. This general thrust is confirmed by the composite scores for each of the samples listed in rank order of the combined averages in Table III-5. Once again, the scoring in this case ranged from 100 for "very much in agreement" down to zero for "very different".

It will be seen that only one of these scores was below the median point of 50 and hence slightly in negative balance: 47 in the case of the French public. From there the range, including the French elite, was definitely upward, with the British in top place and the Italians second. Perhaps most interesting of all in view of what has been said about the general belief that elites have less regard for

Table III-3
Image of America (By Regions)

	Elites			Publics		
	Western Europe	The Americas	Japan	Western Europe	The Americas	Japan
Favorable: International						
Working for peace; lessening tensions; attempting to limit armaments	17%	5%	4%	11%	3%	1%
Desire to do good in the world; unselfishness, generous idealism; willingness to help other nations	12	14	17	10	12	10
Making sacrifices to defend freedom; bulwark against communism; willingness to defend our country, region, or U.S. allies	4	2	3	4	2	1
Political and economic power; military strength	6	4	1	6	3	1
Willingness to accept the burdens of world power; thinking of the interests of the world as a whole	2	3	9	2	2	3
Other favorable international mentions	7	4	3	6	4	1
Favorable: Domestic						
Democracy; political institutions; human rights	20	23	10	12	13	11
Industrial and economic strength; technical know-how	18	20	6	13	12	4
High standard of living; fair distribution of wealth	6	6	1	13	6	1
Efficiency and fairness of the American political and socioeconomic systems; capacity for open discussions, self-criticism, and public cooperation	15	16	8	7	12	7
Favorable characteristics of Americans as people: good, warm, sincere, practical, civic-minded, etc.	7	10	3	4	6	2
Other favorable domestic mentions	6	12	2	7	14	2
General: Don't admire anything about the U.S.	12	9	4	12	13	4
Don't know; no answer	7	5	40	21	18	59

	25%	17%	18%	15%	12%	9%
Unfavorable: International						
Politically imperialistic, arrogant; acts as the policemen or arbiter of the world; insists on being Number One	12	17	9	8	12	6
Economic imperialism; exploitation of other nations; self-centered policies regarding trade	6	5	10	5	6	9
Too aggressive; overly fearful of communism; depends too much on military strength; fosters wars by supplying weapons to other nations						
Clumsy, inexperienced, immature in handling international relations; lacks knowledge of and sensitivity toward others; fails to consult, to cooperate	7	7	4	1	4	4
Other unfavorable international mentions	7	10	2	5	6	2
Unfavorable: Domestic						
Racial, civil rights, black, Mexican-American problems; discrimination	19	19	5	18	20	5
Inefficient political and socioeconomic system; inability to deal with domestic problems; socioeconomic inequalities	13	11	1	9	8	2
Corrupt political system (Nixon, Watergate, etc.)	14	10	1	13	9	2
Materialism; cult of the dollar; capitalism	10	2	3	6	2	2
Excessive freedom and permissiveness: crime, assassinations, abortions, divorces, waste, etc.	6	4	2	9	4	2
Unfavorable characteristics of Americans as people: haughty, conceited, arrogant, selfish, insincere, naive, cynical, uncultured	8	4	1	5	4	*
Other unfavorable domestic mentions	3	4	1	2	4	*
General: Don't dislike anything about the U.S.	5	9	8	8	11	4
Don't know; no answer	9	7	37	26	17	53

Table III-4
Mutuality of Interests (By Regions)

| | Elites | | | Publics | | |
	Western Europe	The Americas	Japan	Western Europe	The Americas	Japan
Very much in agreement	15%	25%	5%	13%	22%	4%
Fairly well in agreement	61	46	58	57	42	47
Rather different	18	17	28	17	20	29
Very different	4	9	2	6	12	4
Don't know	2	3	7	7	4	16

Table III-5
Mutuality of Interests (By Countries)
(Composite Scores)

	Elites	Publics	Combined Averages
Britain	70	69	70
Italy	66	66	66
Germany	65	62	63
Canada	69	55	62
Mexico	62	55	59
Brazil	58	58	58
Japan	57	54	55
France	52	47	50
Overall Averages	62	58	60

the United States than peoples, is that the overall average for the elites at the bottom of Table III-5 is significantly higher than that for the combined publics. The public scores were especially lower than those for the elites in France, Mexico, and particularly Canada. On the other hand, the ratings given by the two types of samples were not statistically different among the British, Italians, and Brazilians.

Since most of those knowledgeable about international relations would probably concede that a sense of mutuality of interests is generally more important than "popularity" in motivating the behavior of nations, it is, of course, reassuring that the overall composite scores in most cases evidenced a positive sense that the basic interest of their own countries were at least fairly well in agreement with those of the United States.

However, how do these current scores compare with past ratings? Designedly, the question on this subject posed in our survey was worded exactly the same as that devised and used by USIA's Office of Research through the years, so that we are in position to chart trends in the case of publics in the four Western European countries surveyed. Taking combined averages at different times, here is how the trends line up.

Publics: Western Europe	
1960	67
1961	66
1967	52
1968	50
1972	67
1974	60

Thus the current figure is well above the depths, previously referred to, in 1967 and 1968, but lower than during the highs of the early 1960s and most recently in 1972. Our suspicion is that the drop during the last two years was occasioned, primarily but not exclusively, by developments in the Middle East and the resulting oil shortages, with which American diplomacy was, no doubt, intimately connected in the minds of Europeans. In fact, for a time the motivation of Western Europeans seemed to be "every country for itself" rather than "we're all, including the United States, in the same boat."

Nevertheless, for the most part the current combined average remained definitely on the positive side—far above where it had been at certain times in the past—indicating a fairly widespread feeling of mutuality of interests.

Cooperating with the United States
Regarding World Shortages

Despite their independent actions during the oil crisis, both elites and publics in all the countries surveyed, including most significantly France, felt, in principle at least, that it would be in their own best interests to work closely with the United States in facing such problems.

> QUESTION: *Turning to another subject, in dealing with world scarcities and high prices of oil and other raw materials, to what extent do you think it would be in (respondent's country's) best interests to cooperate very closely with the United States—a great deal, a fair amount, not very much, or not at all?*

The overall results, grouped on a regional basis are given in Table III-6.

Converting these figures into composite scores (ranging from 100 for "great deal" answers to zero for "not at all"), the results by countries are listed in Table III-7, arranged in the rank order of combined averages, obtained by adding the elite and public ratings and dividing by two.

The lowest scores of all (in France, Brazil, and Japan) were still well above the median point of 50, showing a preponderant view that cooperating with America would prove at least slightly beneficial. In the top range, obviously, were the ratings in Britain, Germany, Canada, and Mexico. More modest enthusiasm was evident in Italy.

Conforming with their greater overall sense of mutuality of interests, the overall average for the elites as a whole was at least slightly higher than that for the publics. This finding is particularly encouraging because the top socio-

Table III-6
Benefit from Cooperating with the United States (By Regions)

	Elites			Publics		
	Western Europe	The Americas	Japan	Western Europe	The Americas	Japan
Great deal	38%	39%	11%	30%	32%	7%
Fair amount	34	34	49	36	36	34
Not very much	17	17	26	15	17	32
Not at all	7	7	2	7	10	4
Don't know	4	3	12	12	5	23

Table III-7
Benefit from Cooperating with the United States (By Countries)
(Composite Scores)

	Elites	Publics	Combined Averages
British	78	75	77
German	78	76	77
Mexican	75	71	73
Canadian	75	65	70
Italian	61	59	60
Brazilian	58	59	59
French	58	55	57
Japanese	59	52	56
Overall Averages	68	64	66

economic groups customarily have more influence on governmental decisions about such economic problems as world scarcities than the peoples as a whole.

Closeness of Relations with the United States

Turning from these generally positive results on mutuality of interests, on the one hand, and benefits from cooperating with the United States, on the other, to the more intimate matter of current relations between their own countries and America, the picture that emerged from our samples as a whole was spotty and in several respects somewhat disquieting. The question involved was the following:

> QUESTION: *Do you feel that relations between the United States and (respondent's country) at present are too close, not close enough, or about right?*

Variations between countries were so great in this case that the voluminous results must be given in detail in Table III-8.

These figures can be looked at in several different ways. To start with, there is the encouraging fact that in the case of every sample the view that relations with the United States are "about right" was predominant, tending to demonstrate that there is at least reasonable satisfaction with the status quo.

On the other hand, the "not close enough" percentages markedly exceeded the "too close" proportions only in Britain and Germany. These were the only samples among whom considerable proportions tended to look with favor on greater intimacy with the United States and Americans. In contrast, the figures in these two opposed respects among both samples in France and Canada, along with the Mexican elite and Italian public, were very close, indeed, indicating a real ambivalence. And the "too close" proportions were decisively greater than the "not close enough" in the case of both samples in Brazil and Japan, and among the Italian elite and Mexican public.

In short, while there was general satisfaction with the present situation, if there were to be any change, opinion among these groups would not want it to come in the direction of greater closeness—or, to put the matter more bluntly, more cloying ties with the American colossus.

Future Relations with the United States

To get at what our samples thought was likely to happen in the future, regardless of their preferences, the following question was posed immediately after the one discussed above:

Table III-8
Desired Proximity to the United States

	Too Close	Not Close Enough	About Right	Don't Know
Elites				
British	6%	29%	65%	*
French	20	25	50	5
German	10	26	60	4
Italian	37	21	40	2
Canadian	22	27	48	3
Mexican	21	21	46	2
Brazilian	40	11	46	3
Japanese	27	16	51	6
Publics				
British	5	30	62	3
French	17	20	51	12
German	8	26	62	4
Italian	26	25	36	13
Canadian	23	23	50	4
Mexican	33	11	52	4
Brazilian	31	17	45	7
Japanese	33	14	41	12

QUESTION: *Do you think that over the next five years relations between the United States and this country will become closer, less close, or stay about the same as they are now?*

The results are given on a country-by-country basis in Table III-9.

These voluminous figures are somewhat difficult to analyze, particularly when it comes to correlating them with the results on the question discussed in the preceding section about whether current relations with the United States are too close, not close enough, or about right. However, there are two main thrusts in this regard.

First, the predominant opinion in most cases was that relations with the United States in the future would remain "about the same"—which would obviously be in accordance with the general desire to maintain the status quo expressed on the preceding question about current relations. The exceptions were in the case of both samples in Mexico and the public samples in Italy and Brazil, where the "closer" figures exceeded "about the same" responses. However, all the other samples had a feeling of stability in the way of a continuation of present relationships with America about as they now are.

Table III-9
Expectations about Future Relations with United States

	Closer	Less Close	About the Same	Don't Know
Elites				
British	20%	19%	56%	5%
French	30	13	45	12
German	19	15	62	4
Italian	37	14	37	12
Canadian	30	23	42	5
Mexican	45	11	40	4
Brazilian	33	13	49	5
Japanese	21	14	53	12
Publics				
British	36	10	47	7
French	24	12	44	20
German	19	11	62	8
Italian	38	10	34	18
Canadian	28	20	48	4
Mexican	47	9	39	5
Brazilian	42	11	38	9
Japanese	15	14	53	18

On the other hand, considerable proportions of some of our respondents felt their desires were going to be frustrated by future developments. This was particularly true among both samples in Mexico and the public in Brazil. Here very substantial proportions felt that relations with the United States were already "too close," but far larger percentages anticipated that, against their wishes, such relationships would become even closer as time went on. This, of course, is a danger signal for the United States, particularly in its dealings with these two countries, whose peoples obviously don't want to feel they are being suffocated by the American presence.

American Corporations

It is probable that a good many sophisticated people believe that American multinational corporations are generally regarded as harmful and potentially dangerous by people abroad. With a very high degree of uncertainty (as indicated by large "don't know" percentages), this was the case with respect to most of our public samples; but not of the majority of the elites. In fact, the overall balance of assessments was on the favorable side—very slightly so, to be sure, but nevertheless definitely not adverse. Here are the questions from which we were able to draw these deductions:

QUESTIONS: *What about American controlled business and industries operating in this country? Would you say that, on the whole, they are benefiting or harming our national interests? Do you think they are benefiting (harming) our interests a great deal or only somewhat?*

The results groups regionally are to be found in Table III-10.

Carrying this further, Table III-11 gives composite scores on a country-by-

Table III-10
Assessments of American Corporations (By Regions)

	Elites			Publics		
	Western Europe	The Americas	Japan	Western Europe	The Americas	Japan
Benefiting a great deal	19%	27%	5%	20%	23%	3%
Benefiting somewhat	30	27	32	23	24	23
Harming somewhat	13	18	17	14	18	16
Harming a great deal	20	18	6	16	24	6
Don't know	18	10	40	27	11	52

Table III-11
Assessments of American Corporations (By Countries)
(Composite Scores)

	Elite	Public	Combined Averages
Britain	60	64	62
Brazil	56	61	58
Mexico	62	48	55
Italy	52	54	53
Japan	53	49	51
Germany	50	49	50
Canada	52	43	48
France	49	44	47
Overall Averages	54	52	53

country basis, arranged in rank order of the combined averages, which were calculated by adding the score for the elite and that of the public in each country and dividing by two. In this case, "benefiting a great deal" answers were weighted at 100, "benefiting somewhat" at two-thirds of 100, "harming somewhat" at one-third and "harming a great deal" at zero.

It will be observed that in the case of the public samples the ratings were below 50, and hence negative, to a very slight degree in Mexico, Japan, and Germany, and more markedly so in Canada and France. But they were positive in Italy and extremely so in Britain and Brazil. As a result the overall composite score for the publics in all eight countries came to a slightly favorable 52.

Most interestingly, the ratings among the more sophisticated socioeconomic elites were uniformly favorable (i.e., above 50) except in Germany and France, in Italy, Japan and Canada to a modest extent, but in Brazil and particularly Britain and Mexico markedly so. The resultant overall score for all the elites was a comfortable 54.

It would thus appear that American corporations abroad are not the albatrosses around our necks that some Americans have seemed to imagine them to be—that is, not yet at least, leaving open the question of what the future may bring as the result chiefly of economic trends.

IV America's International Role, Objectives, and Leadership

We turn now to some more specialized, and in certain cases controversial, aspects of attitudes about the United States: opinions of its role on the world scene, impressions of American motivations and objectives, confidence in U.S. leadership, and reactions to vigorous American participation in international affairs.

Opinions of the U.S. Role Internationally

Most significantly, while not favorable at this stage, assessments of the international role of the United States were relatively less adverse than opinions about America and Americans in general. This is surprising for two reasons: First, as has been observed by most pollsters, the more generalized the subject asked about, the less critical opinions customarily tend to be; the more specific, the more relatively unfavorable. Secondly, in this particular case we found in Chapter III that the image of America and Americans in regard to domestic matters tended, on balance, to be considerably more favorable than that about international items.

How it comes about that attitudes about the international role of the United States are less unfavorable than opinions about our country in general remains something of a mystery. We can only surmise that the generalized bias we found against the United States was a reflection primarily of the irrational, often irritable, love-hate ambivalence which tends to characterize overall attitudes about "America." However, when our foreign respondents were pinned down to a more specific evaluation (i.e., of America's international role) they were forced to think a bit rather than reacting largely emotionally.

Whatever the explanation, the question having to do with matters international was as follows:

QUESTION: *Everything considered, what is your opinion of the role the United States is playing in international affairs and on the world scene generally at the present time—excellent, good, only fair, or poor?*

Table IV-1 gives the results, with the four Western European countries and the three countries in the Americas, respectively, combined, and Japan standing alone.

The composite scores in this case were obtained by rating "excellent" answers at 100; "good" at two-thirds of 100; "only fair" at one-third; and "poor" at zero. The country-by-country scores are listed in Table IV-2 in the rank order of the combined averages of the public and elite samples in each country.

The only combined averages that were really well above the median point of 50, and hence definitely favorable, were, first, among both British samples and, secondly, the Italian public. In terms of combined averages, the German, Canadian and Brazilian ratings were at or near the 50 point, neither positive nor negative. On the other hand, the Mexican, and particularly the Japanese and French figures were definitely adverse.

U.S. Motivations in International Affairs

Views as to whether America is primarily selfish or unselfish in its approach to international matters varied widely among the countries surveyed. The question eliciting these responses was as follows:

QUESTION: *Some people say the United States is genuinely con-*

Table IV-1
Opinions of U.S. International Role (By Regions)

	Elites			Publics		
	Western Europe	The Americas	Japan	Western Europe	The Americas	Japan
Excellent	7%	7%	7%	9%	11%	2%
Good	42	38	23	40	34	16
Only fair	38	43	50	34	40	39
Poor	11	10	7	8	9	20
Don't know	2	2	13	9	6	23

Table IV-2
Opinions of U.S. International Role (By Countries)
(Composite Scores)

	Elites	Publics	Combined Averages
British	55	57	56
Italian	50	57	54
German	49	51	50
Brazilian	48	54	51
Canadian	49	50	50
Mexican	46	46	46
Japanese	45	33	39
French	38	40	39
Overall Averages	48	49	48

cerned about the welfare of other nations and the good of the world. Others say the United States is only concerned about advancing its own selfish interests. What do you, yourself, feel: that the United States is genuinely concerned about the welfare of other nations, or is only concerned about advancing its own selfish interests?

In Table IV-3, countries in which the results were reasonably similar are grouped.

Obviously, only the British believed predominantly that American motivations are humanitarianly based on the welfare of other nations alone. The lowest figures of all in this respect were to be found in Japan. Conversely, only in Mexico and Brazil combined did the view that U.S. concerns are entirely selfish reach majority proportions.

The most interesting thing, however, is that in all countries but Brazil-Mexico the combined total of "welfare of other nations" and "both" replies amounted to substantial majorities, except among the Japanese public where the proportion was only a slight plurality. Since those replying "both" obviously felt that the welfare of other nations is included as one ingredient in American considerations in making international decisions, it can only be deducted that the great majority of our samples, excluding Mexico and Brazil and to a less extent the Japanese public, were of the opinion that U.S. motivations were at least partially, if not wholly, motivated by humanitarian concerns.

Looked at from this point of view, the rather amazing fact emerges that the elites, who might have been expected to look upon this matter with more

Table IV-3
Motivations of United States Internationally

	Welfare Other Nations	Advancing Own Interests	Both	Don't Know
British				
Elite	45%	20%	34%	1%
Public	50	32	15	3
French, German, Italian				
Elites	13	39	46	2
Publics	15	35	44	6
Canadian				
Elite	31	25	43	1
Public	22	38	37	3
Mexican and Brazilian				
Elites	17	50	30	3
Publics	19	53	22	6
Japanese				
Elite	8	25	54	13
Public	4	32	38	26

cynicism because they are more sophisticated, were actually more generously inclined toward America than the publics as a whole. Taking overall averages for all eight countries, in total 61 percent of the elites gave favorable answers—that is, either "welfare of other countries" or "both"—as compared to 53 percent of the publics.

Any way you look at it the majority of our respondents, both public and elite, had an impression of the United States which was unusually complimentary for any great power. In short, the image of an idealistic America may not be as vivid as it once was, for example, during the Marshall Plan years, but it has by no means vanished.

U.S. Objectives

A similar picture, but with different emphases, emerged when our elite respondents were asked to specify what they felt were America's current objectives and goals.

QUESTION: *What in your view are the principal objectives or goals the United States is trying to attain in the international field?*

In this case the results were sufficiently similar in all countries but Japan to permit us to give combined percentages for the seven. Mentions amounting to at least 5 percent by the elites in these countries, along with the corresponding Japanese replies, are given in Table IV-4.

Items having to do with maintaining or achieving strength or power of different sorts, (the first four items in Table IV-4) dominated ideas about the goals of the United States. Superficially, this might appear adverse, but it leaves open the question of the ends toward which respondents thought the powers

Table IV-4
U.S. Objectives (Elites)

	Seven Country Averages	Japan
To be the most powerful nation politically; maintain political hegemony	9%	7%
To maintain maximum economic power or supremacy; dominate the world's economy; enrich itself	28	12
To remain the top nation in military power	5	4
To attain or retain world leadership in power *in general*; to try to dominate the world; control all countries	22	12
	64%	35%
To seek world peace, unity, harmony among all nations; reduce tensions; limit armaments	29%	17%
To preserve democracy; stop Communist expansion; maintain balance of power	8	8
To resolve the problems of the Middle East; overcome the oil and energy crises	5	1
To further the well-being of other countries; provide help to underprivileged nations; promote the world's welfare	5	2
To maintain or increase world economic stability; encourage international trade; stimulate world economic development	5	2
	52%	30%

involved would be used. Judging from the results discussed in the preceding section, it would appear that the elites felt that, on balance, American power would be employed with two intermingled motivations in mind: promoting the welfare of other nations and advancing America's own self-interests. The other items in the rest of Table IV-4, and particularly the goal of achieving world peace, would seem to support this view.

Obviously, as on most subjects, the Japanese had much less to say on this question than respondents in other countries, resulting in large part from the fact that the "don't know" percentage in Japan (45 percent) was five times the average in the others (9 percent). Although this reflects a general tendency customarily evident in polling in Japan, it probably has a particular significance in this case: namely, that, especially because of developments during the Nixon Administration, the Japanese are having particular difficulty these days trying to figure out what America is really up to.

Several variations in particular countries, not evident in Table IV-4, were both interesting and important. For example, the French and particularly the Mexicans put the greatest emphasis on America trying to maximize its *economic* power, with the French also stressing the world leadership aspect. The British elite mentioned both preserving democracy and particularly seeking world peace with frequencies far greater than elsewhere. Conversely, the most infrequent references to these two items occurred in the case of our Latin American neighbors, the Mexicans and Brazilians. The British and Canadians stressed both the well-being of other countries and the attainment of world economic stability as American goals with at least double the frequency prevalent in other countries.

America's Understanding and Consideration

The motivation, objectives, and goals of the United States may be viewed as at least tolerable, if not entirely laudable. But the following question on the extent to which the United States shows understanding and concern for each of the countries surveyed proved to be controversial, eliciting a motley of views.

> QUESTION: *To what extent do you think the United States really tries to understand and take into account (respondent's country's) best interests—a great deal, a fair amount, not very much, or not at all?*

Again grouping the nations in Western Europe, The Americas, and Japan, respectively, the percentaged results came out as shown in Table IV-5.

In Table IV-6 the composite scores, under a system which ranged from 100

Table IV-5
Extent of U.S. Understanding and Consideration (By Regions)

	Elites			Publics		
	Western Europe	The Americas	Japan	Western Europe	The Americas	Japan
Great deal	8%	12%	2%	8%	16%	1%
Fair amount	37	22	29	43	23	19
Not very much	38	49	47	28	44	44
Not at all	14	12	5	11	10	6
Don't know	3	5	17	10	7	30

Table IV-6
Extent of U.S. Understanding and Consideration (By Countries)
(Composite Scores)

	Elites	Publics	Combined Averages
German	58	56	57
British	50	59	55
Italian	48	55	52
Mexican	51	53	52
Brazilian	43	50	47
Japanese	45	40	43
Canadian	40	45	43
French	30	33	32
Overall Averages	46	49	48

for "great deal" to zero for "not at all," are listed in rank order of the combined averages, which were obtained by adding the scores for the public and the elite in each of the countries and then dividing by two.

It will be noted that the combined averages were at least slightly on the favorable side (that is, above the 50 mark) in Germany, Britain, Italy, and Mexico. However they were slightly below the median in Brazil, and even more so in Japan and Canada. In the case of France, the ratings from both samples can only be considered highly adverse.

These results are only what might be expected in a situation in which the United States in recent years has, to a considerable extent, failed to consult with other countries—that is, to listen—when crucial issues were at stake.

Desired U.S. Policies and Actions

Whether our respondents believed the United States tended to be understanding and considerate of their own country's interests or not, it seemed desirable to put the following question to the elite samples in order to find out what policies or actions they felt would, in fact, be best for their own countries.

> QUESTION: *What kinds of American policies and actions in the international field do you, yourself, feel would be in the best interests of this country?*

The results, again grouped regionally, are given in Table IV-7.

Perhaps the most surprising aspect of these results is that the items having to do with improving relations with China and the Soviet Union received such

Table IV-7
Desired U.S. Policies and Actions (Elites)

	Western Europe	The Americas	Japan
Improving relations with mainland China	3%	1%	1%
Improving relations with the USSR: detente	7	1	1
Working for world peace and unity in general; limitation of armaments	16	3	4
Solving Middle Eastern problems in general	8	2	*
Improving the world economic and monetary situation; combating world inflation; dealing with energy problems	14	9	12
Improving economic relations with respondent's own country or region on fair terms; investing or purchasing from own country or region	13	25	10
Protecting respondent's own country or region; keeping Communist threat under control; defending freedom, democracy	19	3	7
Maintaining friendly association with respondent's own country or region; more consultation, mutual cooperation	3	10	2
Increasing U.S. aid to underdeveloped nations	3	3	2
Stop intervening in or interfering with other countries; less imperialism; stop using the CIA	3	14	1

relatively little attention. The same was true, except in the Western European countries, of the more general items having to do with working for world peace and unity and protecting respondent's own country or region. Apparently the sense of imminent threat so pervasive not too long ago has largely dissipated, especially outside Western Europe.

Quite clearly, on an across-the-board basis, the two economic subjects received the major play: improving the world economic and monetary situation and bettering economic relations with respondent's own country or region. Emphasis on economics, it would appear, is the name of the game these days.

A few other items need comment. In the first place, the relatively high frequency with which stopping intervention in or interference with other countries was mentioned in the three countries in the Americas is noteworthy: 12 percent in Brazil, 9 percent in Mexico, and no less than 20 percent among the Canadians, who are tired of feeling engulfed by the United States. At the same time, in these very same cases, the desire for the United States to maintain friendly relations with their own countries or regions was expressed at a higher level than in either Western Europe or Japan. In other words, what the countries in this hemisphere seem to want is less interference and intervention but more friendly association.

Incidentally, even many of supposedly sophisticated members of these elite groups were stumped by this question. The "don't knows" ranged close to two out of ten in Western Europe, one-quarter in the Americas, and no less than two-thirds in Japan. That such a great majority of the Japanese elites should not know what they would like in the way of American policies and actions in today's world seems little short of incredible.

Soviet-American Relations

Assessments of the current state of U.S. relations with the Soviet Union, in general, were by no means euphoric.

> QUESTION: *At the present time, is it your impression that relations between the United States and the Soviet Union are excellent, good, only fair, or poor?*

The combined results for the four Western European countries and the three countries in the Americas, respectively, along with those for Japan, are in Table IV-8.

A plurality of the Japanese public and majorities of all the other groups sampled felt that current relations between the two superpowers were only fair. Turning to composite scores (with "excellent" answers scored at 100 points; "good" at two-thirds of 100; "only fair" at one-third and "poor" at zero) the

Table IV-8
Current State of United States-Soviet Relations

	Elites			Publics		
	Western Europe	The Americas	Japan	Western Europe	The Americas	Japan
Excellent	1%	4%	1%	1%	3%	*
Good	32	28	11	24	19	10
Only fair	60	55	58	56	56	49
Poor	4	6	20	8	10	24
Don't know	3	7	10	11	12	17

ratings, which need not be given in detail, ranged among the elites from 31 in Japan to 48 in Germany; and among the publics from 28 in Japan to 45 in Italy. In other words, all scores were below the median point of 50, indicating once again that each and every sample believed that relations between the United States and the Soviet Union were "only fair" at best.

This is a most significant commentary on assessments of the current "detente." In short, the bulk of our respondents did not consider it something to be heavily relied on, at least not yet.

On the other hand, only small minorities believed that relations between America and Russia were likely to get worse.

> QUESTION: *Over the next few years, do you expect relations between the United States and the Soviet Union will get better, get worse, or stay about the same as they are now?*

The results will be found in Table IV-9.

Table IV-9
Expected Trends in United States-Soviet Relations

	Elites			Publics		
	Western Europe	The Americas	Japan	Western Europe	The Americas	Japan
Relations between United States and Soviets will:						
Get better	39%	43%	15%	34%	40%	15%
Get worse	6	8	5	6	12	8
Stay the same	48	40	64	44	35	52
Don't know	7	9	16	16	13	25

Thus the preponderant view in Western Europe and especially Japan was that relations would remain about the same, with substantial minorities in Western Europe believing that they would get better. And pluralities in the three countries in the Americas actually opted, by narrow margins to be sure, for the "get better" expectation. It is thus clear that our major allies and neighbors do not expect any real crunch between America and the Soviet Union over the next few years. This feeling, of course, helps diminish any sense of threat deriving from a collision between the two.

Fear of United States Favoring Soviets over Respondent's Country

At least for a while a good many commentators were implying that there was a vague but generalized fear abroad, especially in Western Europe, that America might sell its allies down the river in order to make deals with the Soviet Union. With a couple of exceptions, however, this apprehension does not appear to have been at all acute.

QUESTION: *How much danger do you think there is that the United States, in trying to improve relations with the Soviet Union, will take steps or reach agreements which would not be in (respondent's country's) best interests—a great deal, a fair amount, not very much, or none at all?*

The regional results are given in Table IV-10.

To understand deviations among countries on these results, we shall again resort to composite scores, in this case weighting "great deal" answers at 100; "fair amount" at two-thirds of 100; "not very much" at one-third; and "none at

Table IV-10
Extent of Danger of United States Favoring Soviets (By Regions)

	Elites			Publics		
	Western Europe	The Americas	Japan	Western Europe	The Americas	Japan
Great deal	9%	17%	3%	7%	20%	2%
Fair amount	35	25	25	28	29	28
Not very much	37	30	44	34	22	35
None at all	13	22	8	12	16	5
Don't know	6	6	20	19	13	30

all" at zero. The results on this basis are given in Table IV-11 in the rank order of the combined averages.

We will have to adjust our thinking in interpreting the scores in this particular case because figures below the median point of 50, showing a tendency *not* to fear the United States will overcompensate the Soviet Union, must be considered favorable, while those above the median point, showing at least "a fair amount" of such fear, must be construed as adverse.

Obviously on this basis the overall averages, both of which are below 50, cannot be considered unfavorable. The only real feeling of apprehension in this regard was to be found in France, particularly among the elite, and oddly enough in Mexico, especially in the case of the public. In the French situation this probably reflects a basic mistrust of the United States in the international field. The Mexicans, on the other hand, might easily feel that they have been let down, if not sold out by the United States on enough occasions in their history, that they aren't sure they can rule out the possibility of this happening again.

Confidence in U.S. Leadership

Yet even the Mexicans wholeheartedly joined the majority of elites and publics in the countries surveyed in expressing considerable confidence in the ability of America to take the lead in international matters.

QUESTION: *Turning to another subject, how much confidence do you have in the ability of the United States to provide wise leadership in dealing with world problems—a great deal, a fair amount, not very much, or none at all?*

Table IV-11
Extent of Danger of United States Favoring Soviets (By Countries)
(Composite Scores)

	Elites	Publics	Combined Averages
Mexican	54	65	60
French	60	51	55
Brazilian	43	49	46
British	43	46	45
German	45	46	45
Canadian	42	48	45
Japanese	43	46	44
Italian	41	41	41
Overall Averages	46	49	48

The results in percentages, grouped in a regional way, are to be found in Table IV-12.

As usual, the composite scoring system in this case ranged from 100 for "great deal" answers to zero for "none at all". These scores, arranged in rank order of combined averages (obtained by adding the public and elite ratings in each country and dividing by two), are given in Table IV-13.

The ratings of confidence in United States leadership were remarkably favorable in Mexico, Germany, and Great Britain; moderately positive in Italy, Canada, and among the Japanese elite; and adverse (that is, below the median point of 50) only in Brazil and France. Despite the latter two exceptions, it can only be said that the United States did amazingly well on this trust and confidence question, considering the relative uncertainty that prevails today about the international situation in general and America's role in the world in particular.

Table IV-12
Degree of Confidence in United States Leadership (By Regions)

	Elites			Publics		
	Western Europe	The Americas	Japan	Western Europe	The Americas	Japan
Great deal	11%	20%	10%	14%	18%	3%
Fair amount	44	36	48	46	36	41
Not very much	31	29	30	24	27	34
None at all	12	12	3	8	12	5
Don't know	2	3	9	8	7	17

Table IV-13
Degree of Confidence in United States Leadership (By Countries)
(Composite Scores)

	Elites	Publics	Combined Averages
Mexican	63	61	62
German	58	61	60
British	54	62	58
Italian	52	59	56
Canadian	55	56	56
Japanese	57	50	54
Brazilian	48	47	48
French	45	48	47
Overall Averages	54	56	55

In terms of trends, the current composite scores for the publics in Britain, France, Italy, and Germany were exactly, or almost exactly the same as the Institute for International Social Research found in a similar series of studies in 1968. On the other hand, the Japanese score has shifted from a mildly unfavorable 46 to a neutral 50 during this seven-year period.

Vigorous U.S. Role on International Scene

There was strong majority sentiment among our elite samples that the United States will not abate its vigorous international role in the foreseeable future.

> QUESTION: *Over the next five years or so, do you think the United States will continue to play as vigorous a role on the international scene as it has in the past, or do you expect it to reduce its role in world affairs?*

Table IV-14 gives the regional results, which are all that are needed in this case because there was remarkable uniformity from country to country in both Western Europe and the Americas, respectively.

Although the "will continue" percentage in Japan appears much lower than elsewhere, this is chiefly because there were as usual, so many more "don't knows" among the Japanese. In fact, if the figures are percentaged on the basis of those with opinions, the proportion believing the United States will not reduce its international role comes out in Japan to 68 percent, very nearly up to the overall level in Western Europe and the Americas.

In short, despite indications of Americans turning inward, the elite among our major allies and neighbors very evidently do not expect a significant return to isolationism on the part of the United States.

Reactions to this expectation of continued vigor were sharply mixed, however.

Table IV-14
Continuation of Vigorous United States International Role

	Elites		
	Western Europe	The Americas	Japan
Will continue	74%	72%	56%
Will reduce role	21	24	26
Don't know	5	4	18

QUESTION: *Whatever you think may actually happen, would you, yourself, like to see the United States continue to play a vigorous role on the international scene generally, or to reduce its role in world affairs?*

In this case the country-by-country differences were so great that the complete figures have to be given in Table IV-15.

In the case of all samples except the British, the percentages wanting the United States to continue a vigorous international role were *lower* than the proportions thinking that this is actually what the United States will, in fact, do. In other words, except in Britain, expectations were more widespread than desires in this regard.

Within this general framework, however, large majorities of the German, Canadian, and especially British elites hoped the United States would continue with unabated vigor in the international field. The majorities were smaller in Brazil and Italy, and dropped to a mere plurality in Japan. In contrast, however, one-half of the Mexicans and almost that proportion of the French expressed the wish that America would reduce its international role, but with very sizable minorities, nevertheless, opting for continued vigor.

Preferences Regarding American Regional Influence

These variations in views about the continuation of a vigorous U.S. role on the international scene naturally reflected themselves in attitudes towards America's influence in different regions of the world.

Table IV-15
Preferences Regarding U.S. International Role (Elites)

| | Would prefer United States to: | | |
	Continue Vigorous Role	Reduce Its Role	Don't Know
British	83%	14%	3%
French	45	48	7
German	69	25	6
Italian	51	44	5
Canadian	68	27	5
Mexican	45	50	5
Brazilian	53	35	12
Japanese	46	28	26

QUESTION: *Would you like to see the influence of the United States in (respondent's region) increase, decrease, or remain at about the present level?*

The regions referred to in the respective questions were "Western Europe" in the case of the British, French, German, and Italian respondents; "North and South America" in Canada; "Latin America" in the query posed to the Mexicans and Brazilians; and "Asia" vis-à-vis the Japanese. The results, grouped accordingly, are given in Table IV-16.

Clearly, the preponderance of opinion in Western Europe was that American influence should remain at the present level. On the basis of detailed figures not given in Table IV-16, this feeling was especially strong among the British and the Germans, but below average (although still in plurality proportions) in the case of the Italian public. On the other hand, the Italian elite preponderantly wanted the influence of the United States to decrease, and the French elite was split almost evenly between "decrease" and "present level."

With considerably less conviction, pluralities of both Japanese samples wanted American influence in Asia to remain at the present level, but this sentiment was weak, to say the least, in the case of the public. In fact, in both Japanese samples approximately three out of ten respondents opted for "decrease" in this regard.

In Canada, Mexico, and Brazil combined, on the other hand, the publics were pretty evenly divided among the three options "increase," "decrease," or "remain at the present level." But the elites came in preponderantly for lessened influence in this hemisphere, a sentiment which was especially pronounced among elite Brazilians.

Thus this issue of America's influence in these various parts of the world proved to be very controversial to say the least.

Table IV-16
Preferences Regarding America's Regional Influence

	Elites			Publics		
	Western Europe	The Americas	Japan	Western Europe	The Americas	Japan
Increase	13%	19%	14%	20%	28%	7%
Decrease	35	46	29	22	33	31
Present level	50	29	46	49	31	39
Don't know	2	6	11	9	8	23

V Attitudes Toward the Soviet Union and China

We also thought it useful to see how our major allies and neighbors felt about our former "enemies" and—despite "detente"—still potential adversaries, the USSR and mainland China. The idea was not to conduct some kind of popularity contest, but rather to find out, in the wake of President Richard M. Nixon's initiatives toward Russia and China, what psychological transformations may have occurred in this period of transition in world affairs.

The questions involved in this chapter were worded the same as the related ones about the United States and will not be repeated here.

Opinions of the USSR and China

Respondents were asked for their opinion of each of the two powers, its policies and actions. The composite scores that emerged are given in Table V-1. It will be recalled that in this case "excellent" answers were rated at 100 points; "good" at two-thirds of 100; "only fair" at one-third; and "poor" at zero.

The first thing to be noted is that opinion ratings across-the-board given both powers were below the median point of 50, hence in the negative range. There was this important difference however: the adverse balances were relatively modest in the case of China, but decidedly pronounced in regard to the Soviet Union. Within this general frame of reference, the Japanese combined averages in regard to the Soviet Union were markedly below the overall average for all the samples surveyed.

With regard to China, the combined averages were actually at or slightly below the 50 mark in France and Germany; but, again, quite well below the

Table V-1
Opinions of the USSR and China
(Composite Scores)

	Soviet Union			China		
	Elites	Publics	Combined Averages	Elites	Publics	Combined Averages
British	35	39	37	46	44	45
French	36	41	39	50	49	50
German	36	32	34	51	51	51
Italian	38	40	39	51	40	46
Canadian	39	36	38	50	43	47
Mexican	37	41	39	43	40	42
Brazilian	40	39	40	42	40	41
Japanese	25	22	24	38	36	37
Overall Averages	36	36	36	46	43	45

overall average for all samples in the case of Japan, although not as profoundly so as with regard to Russia.

In short, neither of these powers proved popular anywhere, especially not among the Japanese. To put this matter in perspective, however, we must compare the overall averages obtained from all the samples in regard to opinions of the USSR and China with those of the United States given in Chapter III.

	Elites	Publics	Combined Averages
The Soviet Union	36	36	36
China	46	43	45
United States	41	43	42

The interesting fact emerges that, while the Soviet Union was quite far behind, China actually nosed out the United States among the combined elites and equaled the United States in the case of the publics. As a result, China's combined score for both types of samples ended up higher than that for America. Thus we shall have to modify the statement made above with respect to the Soviet Union and China by saying that, not only they, but the United States is really not popular these days.

Mutuality of Interests with the USSR

The views of our samples about mutuality of interests with the Soviet Union were even more adverse than their opinions of the country itself. It will be recalled that the question in this regard asked whether respondents felt the basic interests of the Soviet Union and those of their own country were "very much in agreement" (weighted under our scoring system at 100), "fairly well in agreement" (weighted at two-thirds of 100), "rather different" (weighted at one-third of 100), or "very different" (weighted at zero). The composite scores so calculated are given in Table V-2 in rank order of the combined averages.

In short, with somewhat limited exceptions in the case of Italy and Canada, the composite scores from all samples were decidedly negative, showing that our respondents had little feeling of mutuality of interest with the Soviet Union. This was especially true in Mexico, Brazil, and Japan, as the combined averages indicate.

This is obviously a heavy cross the Soviet Union will have to bear. It is difficult to promote cooperation on any broad scale in the absence of mutual feelings that interests are substantially in agreement. The extent to which America has an advantage in this respect is typified by the differences between the ratings assigned the two powers on mutuality of interests. The overall averages for all samples were as follows:

	Elites	Publics	Combined Averages
The USSR	34	34	34
The United States	62	58	60

It is, above all, in this area of mutual feeling that America and Americans still maintain a definite advantage.

Table V-2
Mutuality of Interests with USSR
(Composite Scores)

	Elites	Publics	Combined Averages
Italian	41	42	41
Canadian	41	43	42
British	36	39	38
French	37	37	37
German	34	32	33
Mexican	27	28	27
Brazilian	27	26	27
Japanese	26	27	27
Overall Averages	34	34	34

Japan's Mutuality of Interests with China

Because mainland China is so much out of the customary orbit of the other countries surveyed, we asked only the Japanese about mutuality of interests with China. It turned out that majorities of both samples (64 percent of the elite; 55 percent of the public) were of the opinion that the basic interests of China were "rather different" or "very different" than the basic interests of their own country. The resultant composite scores were 38 in the case of the elite and 37 for the public. Both of these, obviously, were very low, although higher than the ratings given the Soviet Union in this regard. The comparable Japanese figures for mutuality with the United States, incidentally, were 57 in the case of the elite and 54 among the public.

Perhaps the most interesting thing about the results regarding China is that more than one-quarter of Japan's public and 13 percent of the elite said they didn't know to what degree their country enjoyed mutuality of interests with mainland China—an indication of considerable uncertainty.

Closeness of Relations with China

The replies of our respondents everywhere when asked whether relations between their own country and China were too close, not close enough, or about right, are given in Table V-3.

Looking first at the elite figures in Table V-3, only in Britain and by a huge margin in Japan was there a majority view that relations with China were "not close enough." In plurality proportions this feeling also prevailed in Italy and

Table V-3
Desired Proximity to China

	Elites							
	Britain	France	Germany	Italy	Canada	Mexico	Brazil	Japan
Too close	*%	7%	3%	3%	5%	7%	3%	1%
Not close enough	52	39	45	46	36	20	49	71
About right	42	43	42	40	46	61	36	21
Don't know	6	11	10	11	13	12	12	7

	Publics							
Too close	2	7	2	2	6	10	6	1
Not close enough	39	25	34	28	31	20	41	70
About right	45	39	45	34	45	60	33	17
Don't know	14	29	19	36	18	10	20	12

Brazil. There was a virtual stand-off in France and Germany. In contrast, a large majority of the Mexican elite and a plurality of the Canadian felt that current relations were already "about right," and did not need to become closer.

At the level of public opinion, again a large majority of the Japanese, joined once more by a plurality of the Brazilians, wanted closer relationships with China. In all the other countries surveyed, "about right" sentiment was in the ascendancy at least by modest margins and in Mexico in a majority proportion.

It is interesting to note that the "don't know" percentages among the Japanese on this issue of closer relations with China were far lower than in the case of most other questions asked. Clearly, on this particular matter, the Japanese have made up their minds with a relatively modest degree of uncertainty.

To give a sense of the general thrust of the figures, the across-the-board averages for all eight countries were as follows:

	Elites	Publics
Relations with China Are:		
Too close	4%	4%
Not close enough	45	36
About right	41	40
Don't know	10	20

Thus, by very slight margins, the combined elites leaned toward the "not close enough" view, the publics toward "about right." In effect, then, except in Japan there was no very strong feeling anywhere to move closer to the mainland Chinese.

The results when our samples were asked whether over the next five years relations with China would become closer, less close, or remain about the same are given on a regional basis in Table V-4. In this case the percentages by regions

Table V-4
Future Relations with China

	Elites			Publics		
	Western Europe	The Americas	Japan	Western Europe	The Americas	Japan
Closer	46%	51%	59%	34%	46%	55%
Less close	4	4	6	5	5	6
About the same	38	35	25	36	36	24
Don't know	12	10	10	25	13	15

are sufficient because the general thrust of the results in the various countries in Western Europe and the Americas, respectively, did not differ markedly.

The elites in Western Europe predominantly anticipated closer relations with China. On the other hand, the Western European publics were almost evenly divided between the idea that relations would become closer, on the one hand, or stay about the same, on the other. In contrast, all samples, publics as well as elites, in the Americas tended to look toward closer proximity with China. The Japanese agreed even more heartily, again with relatively low "don't know" percentages.

Closeness of Relations with the USSR

The regional figures as to whether relations with the USSR are too close, not close enough, or about right are to be found in Table V-5.

Although the feeling that relations with Russia were not close enough proved to be very considerable (unlike the case vis-à-vis the United States), the predominant preference in the case of all publics and elites in Western Europe was for the situation to stay as it is now. This feeling also prevailed in the three countries in the Americas except that figures not given in Table V-5 show the Brazilian public opted for the "not close enough" alternative by a significant but not large margin. In contrast, the Japanese went overboard in favoring closer proximity to the USSR—decidedly unlike their views in regard to the United States.

However, when it came to the question of whether future relations with Russia would actually become closer, less close, or remain about the same, even the Japanese joined the rest of the samples in preponderantly foreseeing that any significant change was not likely. Table V-6 gives the figures.

Thus a large proportion of the Japanese in particular felt their wish for greater intimacy with the Soviet Union was not going to be fulfilled.

Table V-5
Desired Proximity to the USSR

	Elites			Publics		
	Western Europe	The Americas	Japan	Western Europe	The Americas	Japan
Too close	7%	5%	1%	6%	6%	*
Not close enough	37	32	61	33	31	59
About right	53	56	28	48	52	22
Don't know	3	7	10	13	11	19

Table V-6
Future Relations with the USSR

	Elites			Publics		
	Western Europe	The Americas	Japan	Western Europe	The Americas	Japan
Closer	38%	36%	27%	31%	38%	19%
Less close	6	6	13	6	7	11
About the same	47	49	48	45	44	46
Don't know	9	9	12	18	11	24

Closeness of Relations with Eastern Europe

Generally speaking, our samples exhibited varying proportions in favor of closer relations with "the Eastern European bloc countries, such as Poland, Hungary, and East Germany." The results are listed in Table V-7.

The desire for closer proximity with Eastern Europe was very considerably stronger among the elites than among the publics. Detailed figures not given in Table V-7 show, in fact, that the only country in which the elite opted predominantly for the notion that relations were already about right and didn't need to become closer was Mexico. The Mexican public agreed with this proposition, and the publics in Germany, Italy, and Canada were very close to being evenly divided between the "about right" and the "not close enough" stances. In contrast, the publics in Britain, France, and Brazil were predominantly in favor of closer relations. Japan was the only country, however, in which this sentiment came anywhere near reaching majority proportions.

In general, in the countries surveyed, however, it can be said that there was a considerable reaching out for closer relations with China, the Soviet Union, and Eastern Europe—much more so, in fact, than was the case vis-à-vis the United

Table V-7
Desired Proximity to Eastern Europe

	Elites			Publics		
	Western Europe	The Americas	Japan	Western Europe	The Americas	Japan
Too close	5%	3%	1%	6%	6%	1%
Not close enough	55	44	63	39	36	52
About right	34	39	18	36	40	14
Don't know	6	14	18	19	18	33

States. However, there is, obviously, a vast difference in the situations involved because relations with America are already so close that it would be difficult to conceive of them becoming much closer, short of complete domination by the superpower.

Confidence in Soviet Leadership

As in the case of the United States discussed in Chapter IV, our samples were asked how much confidence they had "in the Soviet Union to provide wise leadership in dealing with world problems." Once again, to avoid the excessive listing of figures we shall rely exclusively in this case on composite scores to give the thrust of the results, with "great deal" answers rated at 100 points; "fair amount" at two-thirds of 100; "not very much" at one-third; and "none at all" at zero. The results so calculated are given in Table V-8, ranked in order of the combined averages.

Several things in Table V-8 are worth noting. To start with, there was slightly more confidence in the Soviet leadership among the publics than the more sophisticated elites. Secondly, even the highest of the scores (in Mexico, Canada, and France) were significantly below the median point of 50, indicating a predominant feeling of "not very much" confidence. The combined average in Brazil was extremely adverse; and so, in fact, were the overall averages across-the-board. The very least that can be said is that there is not much trust in the Soviets when it comes to taking a lead in world affairs.

Table V-8
Confidence in Soviet Leadership
(Composite Scores)

	Elites	Publics	Combined Averages
Mexican	39	46	43
Canadian	41	42	42
French	37	44	41
British	36	42	39
German	38	37	38
Italian	34	41	38
Japanese	39	37	38
Brazilian	32	31	32
Overall Averages	37	40	39

Confidence in Chinese Leadership

The results on a similar question about confidence in Chinese leadership were even more unfavorable than with respect to the Soviet Union. This is evident in Table V-9.

All of the scores except to a limited extent in Japan were far below the median point of 50, indicating very little confidence in the wisdom of the Chinese in international matters. The great exception was that the scores afforded China by the Japanese, while still negative (43 in the case of both samples), were nevertheless higher than the ratings given the Soviet Union (Japanese elite 39; public 37). Thus, comparatively speaking, the Japanese have more (although still not much) trust in China than in Russia.

To give a picture of the relative standings of these two countries compared to that of the United States, it is only necessary to list the overall averages accorded the three on these confidence questions:

	Elites	Publics	Combined Averages
United States	54	56	55
Soviet Union	37	40	39
Mainland China	34	36	35

Thus, whatever the opinions of the United States and its current international role may be, the United States has an enormous advantage over its potential adversaries when it comes to trust and confidence in its leadership in world affairs.

Table V-9
Confidence in Chinese Leadership
(Composite Scores)

	Elites	Publics	Combined Averages
Japanese	43	43	43
French	37	38	38
Mexican	34	42	38
Canadian	36	35	36
German	33	35	34
British	30	34	32
Italian	30	30	30
Brazilian	26	27	27
Overall Averages	34	36	35

VI Power and Importance

In the wake of World War II, the United States found itself the most omnipotent nation in the history of the world. It was perceived as unrivaled Number One in terms of all kinds of power: political, economic, diplomatic, and, since it enjoyed a monopoly of atomic weapons, military above all.

Then things began to change. The Soviet also acquired atomic bombs, as did the British and the French. The Russians launched their Sputnik in 1957, which triggered throughout the world an image of scientific and technological mastery rivaling that of the United States. Shortly after this, it became apparent that Europe had begun to coalesce on a scale unmatched since the Roman Empire, and Germany and Japan especially exhibited great economic and industrial progress.

Later, America's vast military might was stymied by a small Asian nation in Indochina. In 1972 President Nixon journeyed to Peking and Moscow, to set up negotiations with these two powers. The SALT agreements explicitly recognized and legitimized nuclear equivalence, at the least, between the Soviet Union and America.

In a world drastically changed by such developments, the issue naturally arises: What are today's perceptions of the relative importance and power of various nations and groupings of nations, such as the European Economic Community. To get at this, in the course of the interview our respondents were shown a picture of a ladder with steps numbered from zero at the bottom to ten at the top, with the following explanation:

"Now I'd like you to show me on the ladder how much importance and political, economic, or military power you feel each of the countries I am going

to mention has today. A very great power which you consider to be in the very strongest class would be at the top of the ladder; a very small, weak power at the bottom. If you think two countries are of about equal rank, you can put them on the same step."

Those interviewed were asked to indicate where they thought the United States, the Soviet Union, and their own country, respectively, stand on the ladder today; where they stood ten years ago; and where they probably will stand about ten years from now. Present and future (but not past) ratings were also obtained in regard to China, Japan, and "the Western European countries grouped together in the Common Market, including Great Britain, France, West Germany, Italy and five other smaller European nations."

Under this system the highest possible rating would be 10.0; the lowest 0.0.

United States v. USSR: Elite Samples

The average ratings, past, present, and future, given the United States and the Soviet Union, respectively, by the more knowledgeable, sophisticated elite samples are given in Table VI-1.

The overall averages at the bottom of each column were computed in a simplistic way by adding all the scores and then dividing by the number of such scores, not taking into account differences in population, etc.).

In analyzing these results we must bear in mind that, for it to be statistically significant, a change or difference in ratings must amount to at least 0.6 steps on the ladder. Taking this into account, it is apparent that among the socioeconomic elites in all the countries surveyed there were no significant shifts in the

Table VI-1
Power and Importance: United States v. USSR (Elites)

	Ratings Assigned United States			Ratings Assigned USSR		
	Past	Present	Future	Past	Present	Future
British	9.1	8.8	8.5	7.5	8.4	8.6
French	8.7	8.6	8.4	6.6	7.8	8.4
German	8.3	8.1	7.7	6.6	7.7	7.9
Italian	9.2	8.9	8.7	7.0	8.1	8.4
Canadian	8.7	8.6	8.1	7.0	8.2	8.3
Mexican	9.2	9.4	9.1	7.4	8.6	8.9
Brazilian	8.5	8.8	7.8	6.6	7.9	7.8
Japanese	7.8	7.9	7.9	6.5	7.1	7.6
Overall Averages	8.7	8.6	8.3	6.9	8.0	8.2

average ratings assigned the United States from past to present. Similarly, the only shift from present to future large enough to be meaningful was among the Brazilian elite, who saw the United States dropping one full step of the ladder over the next ten years.

However, comparing the elite ratings for ten years before with those for ten years ahead, there were no significant U.S. increases anywhere over the total twenty year span, but significant declines emerged in Britain, Germany, Canada, and Brazil.

On the other hand, every elite sample without exception saw measurable enhancements of Soviet power and importance from past to present in all cases but two (Britain and Japan) exceeding one full step of the ladder. In contrast, from present to future only the French elite anticipated that Soviet prestige would increase significantly during the next ten years.

In short, the great majority of elites anticipated that the next ten years would be a period of essential stability in both U.S. and Soviet power and importance.

Comparing the present ratings assigned the United States with those given the Soviet Union, despite the perceived upward surge of the latter over the past ten years, the United States nevertheless remained significantly ahead in France, Italy, Mexico, Brazil, and Japan. The two were already seen as essentially equivalent in Britain, Germany, and Canada.

Beyond this, looking at the future ratings of the two powers, by ten years from now all concerned believed that essential parity will have been attained by the Soviets.

United States v. USSR: Public Samples

The results from the samples of the general public were basically similar to those from the elites, as can be seen in Table VI-2.

Except for the rise perceived by the Mexican and Brazilian publics, there were no significant shifts in the U.S. ratings from past to present; and from present to future there were no measurable changes anywhere, including Mexico and Brazil.

Conversely, all the publics concerned felt the Soviet Union had risen during the past ten years in all cases but the Japanese by more than one full step of the ladder. From present to future, only the Germans and Italians felt Soviet power and importance would increase significantly.

Nevertheless, over the entire twenty years span from ten years ago to ten years from now, even the Japanese anticipated a total Soviet enhancement of more than one full step, with the rest of the samples registering much more than that.

Comparing the present ratings of the two superpowers, as among the elite samples, the United States remained ahead at present in Italy, Mexico, Brazil, and Japan. But in this case the French public, unlike the elite, joined the British,

Table VI-2
Power and Importance: United States v. USSR (Publics)

	Ratings Assigned United States			Ratings Assigned USSR		
	Past	Present	Future	Past	Present	Future
British	8.5	8.5	8.7	7.0	8.1	8.6
French	8.3	8.5	8.4	6.6	8.0	8.5
German	8.0	7.8	7.5	6.3	7.4	8.0
Italian	8.3	8.5	8.5	6.4	7.7	8.3
Canadian	8.3	8.4	8.0	6.6	8.0	8.3
Mexican	8.0	9.0	9.1	7.0	8.4	8.9
Brazilian	6.8	8.0	7.6	5.0	6.5	6.9
Japanese	7.8	7.8	7.7	6.4	7.1	7.6
Overall Averages	8.0	8.3	8.2	6.4	7.6	8.1

German and Canadian publics in perceiving essential equality even as of now. In all countries surveyed except Brazil a state of equivalence was foreseen by ten years from now.

As shown in a similar Potomac Associates study conducted in the United States under the direction of the author in January 1974, the American public tended to agree with this conclusion about eventual equivalency.[a] Here are the present and future ratings assigned the United States and the USSR, respectively, by Americans:

	United States	USSR
Present	8.8	8.0
Future	7.8	7.9

Thus, while the American sample thought the United States was a full step of the ladder above the Soviet Union as of the time of the survey, they anticipated complete equivalence ten years in the future as a result of a sharp drop in the power and importance of the United States.

Views About Equivalence of Power

Returning to our current surveys, it might seem odd to most Americans that this perceived state of equivalence between the United States and the USSR, whether now or in the future, was not viewed as dangerous by our allies and neighbors. In

[a]See the chapter on "The International Attitudes of Americans" by Lloyd A. Free in A Nation Observed, edited by Donald R. Lesh (Potomac Associates, 1974).

fact, majorities in most of the countries surveyed welcomed it. This is evident from the results on the following question asked after the various ladder ratings for the United States and the Soviet Union had been obtained:

> QUESTION: *Whatever you think may actually happen, which would you personally like to see more powerful ten years from now, the United States or the Soviet Union—or would you rather see them about equal in power?*

The responses are quantified in Table VI-3.

Among the elites, even in Mexico a slight plurality preferred equivalence to American superiority, while among the elites in other countries surveyed this proportion rose to around six out of ten, except in Brazil where, however, it was still of majority proportions.

The thinking of the publics exhibited much the same general thrust. Here

Table VI-3
Preferred Power Alignment: United States v. USSR

	US More Powerful	Soviets More Powerful	About Equal	Don't Know
Elites				
British	37%	1%	61%	1%
French	25	5	62	8
German	35	2	61	2
Italian	30	5	60	5
Canadian	36	2	59	3
Mexican	44	3	47	6
Brazilian	37	2	54	7
Japanese	29	3	59	9
Overall Averages	34%	3%	58%	5%
Publics				
British	49	1	47	3
French	21	6	62	11
German	39	4	51	6
Italian	28	6	54	12
Canadian	30	2	62	6
Mexican	37	8	49	6
Brazilian	42	4	45	9
Japanese	17	5	59	19
Overall Averages	33%	4%	54%	9%

again, except for the British and Brazilian publics, which were split almost down the middle, preponderant feeling among the people of all the countries surveyed opted for equivalence rather than U.S. preponderance.

We can only speculate as to the reasoning behind these results. Our hypotheses are, first, that a situation of rough equivalence—or, put another way, stalemate—may be conceived of as reducing the danger of war between, or adventurousness on the part of either of the two superpowers, thus lessening potential threats to respondents' own countries. Also, among the more sophisticated at least, the feeling may be that more or less equal power will allow more leeway for their own nation to navigate, potentially permitting them even to play one superpower off against the other. Put more bluntly, this preference may arise in part also from sheer aversion to a continuation of the situation which existed after World War II, in which a single nation was Number One throughout the world, largely omnipotent, even though this nation happened to be the United States, which the more sophisticated tended to view in general as unusually benign.

China, Japan, Western Europe

The present and future ratings assigned China, Japan, and the Common Market countries generally make it clear that both publics and elites in all the countries surveyed did not view them as currently in the same league as the United States or the USSR; nor, despite considerable anticipated increases in power and importance, was it felt that they would achieve that status in any complete sense within the next ten years. These findings are shown in Table VI-4.

Remembering again that, for a difference between two ratings to be significant, the spread must amount to at least 0.6 steps of the ladder, the most remarkable fact that emerges from the overall averages in this table is that China, Japan, and the Common Market countries were rated essentially equal both in the present and the future by both the elite and public samples as a whole. This is obviously a great compliment to Japan in view of the fact that China has nuclear weapons and the Western European countries, two of which also possess nuclear capabilities, are an agglomeration of nine nations instead of a single one like Japan.

We have seen above that the average overall rating for the present assigned the United States and the Soviet Union by the elite samples as a whole were 8.6 and 8.0, respectively; and by the public samples 8.3 and 7.6. Compared to these, the overall average ratings in the present for China, Japan, and the Common Market countries that emerged from both the elite and public samples ranged from a mere 6.2 to 6.5, very much lower, indeed. Thus, if the hypothesis of the so-called pentagonal power structure advanced by the Nixon Administration assumes anything even remotely approaching the concept of five roughly

Table VI-4
Power and Importance: China, Japan, Western Europe

	Ratings Assigned to:					
	China		Japan		Common Market	
	Present	Future	Present	Future	Present	Future
Elites						
British	6.2	7.6	5.7	6.0	6.4	7.4
French	6.0	7.4	6.7	7.0	6.3	7.1
German	5.9	7.3	5.7	6.0	6.1	6.8
Italian	6.4	7.6	6.9	7.4	6.3	7.2
Canadian	6.5	7.6	6.4	6.8	6.2	6.6
Mexican	6.9	7.9	7.9	8.5	7.7	8.2
Brazilian	6.2	7.2	7.2	7.5	7.0	7.0
Japanese	6.0	7.1	5.7	6.2	6.0	6.3
Overall Averages	6.3	7.5	6.5	6.9	6.5	7.1
Publics						
British	6.4	7.4	6.1	6.7	6.6	7.5
French	6.5	7.5	6.7	7.0	6.5	7.5
German	5.8	7.3	5.7	6.1	6.1	7.0
Italian	6.1	6.7	6.6	7.3	6.6	7.4
Canadian	6.6	7.5	6.3	6.9	6.2	6.8
Mexican	7.2	8.2	7.6	8.4	7.7	8.3
Brazilian	5.3	6.2	5.9	6.7	6.3	6.6
Japanese	6.0	7.1	5.8	6.3	6.2	6.4
Overall Averages	6.2	7.2	6.3	6.9	6.5	7.2

equivalent power centers, both elite groups and general publics in the countries surveyed rejected this notion.

Looking at the overall future ratings, it is significant that, with the single exception of the elites' prognostications about Japan, both publics and elites saw significant enhancements of these alternative power centers over the next ten years. However, even as of then the overall future ratings assigned China, Japan, and Western Europe given by the two sets of samples ranged from a low of 6.9 in the case of forecasts about Japan to a high of 7.5 for China among the elites and 7.2 for both China and the Common Market countries among the general publics.

Even the highest of these figures are significantly lower than the 8.1 to 8.3 range of the overall future ratings for the United States and the Soviet Union given by both elite groups and general publics as a whole.

Thus, ten years in the future, the world envisioned in the countries surveyed would not be of a single top dog, the United States, but of two top dogs, the United States and the USSR. The Common Market countries, Japan, and China would constitute lesser but nevertheless significant sub-power centers of almost mutually equal importance.

Self-assessments Within the Nations Surveyed

Respondents in each of the countries surveyed were also asked to rate their own nation in terms of power and importance at present, as of ten years ago, and ten years from now. The average ladder ratings that emerged are given in Table VI-5. In studying these it is important to remember that the assessments involved were made exclusively by respondents in each particular country, not by our samples across-the-board as in the case of ratings discussed above.

The first point of interest is that none of the samples saw their own country as enjoying power and importance even remotely approaching that of the United States or the USSR; in short, their own self-assessments were to the effect that their countries were very considerably "inferior" in this respect. This was true even of the Japanese, who placed their own nation very much lower than other samples rated Japan on our earlier question discussed above. It also applied to the French, who very clearly have not swallowed the delusions of grandeur promulgated by their late leaders.

Comparing present with past ratings, the British and Italians felt their nations had declined substantially over the last ten years. The French saw no significant increment in their own power and influence. However, the Germans, Canadians, Mexicans, Japanese, and especially Brazilians pictured substantial, and in some cases, gigantic enhancements in their relative standings.

All samples anticipated some improvement from present to future, and most thought that their nation would be significantly more important and powerful ten years from now than it had been ten years ago. The pessimistic exceptions were the British and Italians, who believed that ten years from now they would still not have regained the stature they had enjoyed twenty years earlier.

However, even the British and Italians wanted improvement in this respect. This emerged when all of our samples were asked the following question:

QUESTION: *In general, would you like (your own country) to gain more power and importance in the world by playing a more active role and taking on more responsibilities internationally, or play a less active role with fewer responsibilities—or are you satisfied with the situation as it now stands?*

Table VI-5
Self-assessments of Power and Importance

	Past	Present	Future
Britain			
Elite	6.4	4.6	5.1
Public	7.0	5.4	6.3
France			
Elite	5.2	5.2	5.6
Public	5.6	5.5	6.3
Germany			
Elite	4.8	5.6	6.1
Public	5.0	5.6	6.1
Italy			
Elite	5.1	3.1	4.1
Public	5.4	3.9	4.9
Canada			
Elite	4.7	5.5	6.3
Public	5.3	6.4	7.3
Mexico			
Elite	4.5	5.4	6.7
Public	5.3	6.4	7.5
Brazil			
Elite	3.4	5.6	7.6
Public	4.1	6.5	7.8
Japan			
Elite	4.8	5.7	6.2
Public	4.8	5.8	6.3

As would normally be expected, majorities, often large, of most samples wanted their own countries to achieve more power and importance even at the expense of taking more responsibilities. The sizes of the selected majorities who desired this are indicated by the following figures:

	Elites	Publics
Mexico	85%	85%
Italy	87	77

	Elites	Publics
Brazil	81	71
France	70	63
Canada	60	66
Britain	53	57

The respondents who showed hesitation about taking on a more active role were to be found to a limited extent among the Japanese public and much more as in the case of both samples in Germany. The detailed figures are as follows:

	Japan		Germany	
	Elite	Public	Elite	Public
Play more active role	61%	50%	47%	42%
Play less active role	3	5	8	9
Satisfied with present situation	26	27	43	44
Don't know	10	18	2	5
	100%	100%	100%	100%

The most interesting feature of this picture in regard to the Japanese public and especially the samples in Germany is that it is precisely these two countries which, from at least the economic point of view, have the best springboard from which to leap up of any of those surveyed. Their hesitation about taking on a more active political role is probably a heritage of their special experience during World War II and the period thereafter.

VII War, Alliances, Defense

Some of the sharpest variations of opinions as between the countries surveyed had to do, on the one hand, with the danger that they themselves might become involved in a damaging war, and, on the other, with the likelihood that a violent nuclear confrontation might occur between the United States and the Soviet Union. The one thing on which they were all in substantial agreement was that, if nuclear war did break out between the two superpowers, injuries to their own people would be colossal.

Danger of War Affecting Own Country

The first question asked along these lines was as follows:

> QUESTION: *How much danger do you think there is that a nuclear war or one not involving nuclear weapons may break out within the next ten years that would bring sorrow or suffering to the people of your country—a great deal, a fair amount, not very much, or none at all?*

Once again, we shall give only the composite scores on this question, calculated on a basis ranging from 100 for "a great deal" to zero for "none at all." The ratings in Table VII-1 are ranked in the order of combined averages, obtained by adding the elite and public scores and dividing by two.

It is interesting to note that all of the scores in the case of the Brazilians and Mexicans were far above the median point of 50, indicating a predominant view

75

**Table VII-1
Danger of War Affecting Own Country
(Composite Scores)**

	Elites	Publics	Combined Averages
Brazilian	76	76	76
Mexican	61	76	69
French	48	49	49
Canadian	45	51	48
British	40	43	42
Italian	30	40	35
German	28	34	31
Japanese	31	31	31
Overall Averages	45	50	48

that there was considerable danger that a war would break out damaging to their own country. The only other score above 50—and, indeed, only very slightly so—was the 51 among the Canadian public. The French ratings similarly hovered around the median point. In contrast, very little fear was expressed by the Italians, Germans, and Japanese, who preponderantly thought there was "not very much" danger of such a war.

Also noteworthy is the fact that the elites were not as fearful of war as the less well informed publics, as indicated by their respective overall averages.

Danger of Nuclear War Between the United States and the USSR

A similar lineup emerged when the question posed had to do with the likelihood of a nuclear confrontation between the two superpowers.

QUESTION: *And how much danger do you feel there is that a full-scale nuclear war may break out between the United States and the Soviet Union within the next ten years?*

The composite scores are given in Table VII-2.

Judging from the respective overall averages, it is apparent, first, that the elites were again more complacent about this subject than the publics and, secondly, that there was significantly less fear among both publics and elites of a

Table VII-2
Danger of Nuclear War Between United States and USSR
(Composite Scores)

	Elites	Publics	Combined Averages
Brazilian	59	70	64
Mexican	48	72	60
French	32	37	35
Canadian	32	35	34
British	26	32	29
Italian	20	33	27
Japanese	26	26	26
Germany	21	26	24
Overall Averages	33	41	37

nuclear war between the United States and the Soviet Union than of a war in general which might damage the countries surveyed.

However, within this context the patterning of responses on this question was almost exactly the same as on the previous one. Once again, the least fearful were the Italians, Japanese, and Germans. And again, only the Brazilians and Mexicans expressed significant fear of a nuclear confrontation. Why these two peoples proved to be so extremist on both of these questions is very difficult for us to surmise.

Bolstering the relatively low combined averages on these two questions is the rather remarkable fact, evident in detailed figures not given in the tables above, that around two out of ten of both the elite and public samples across-the-board thought there was no danger at all of a war breaking out that would affect their own country. Approximately three out of ten thought that there was no danger at all of a nuclear outbreak between the United States and the USSR.

Damage from Nuclear War

The relative relaxation about the likelihood of nuclear war was undoubtedly comforting to our respondents since they all felt that, in the event a nuclear holocaust should occur, their own countries would be devastated.

QUESTION: *If a nuclear war between the United States and the Soviet Union did break out, how much danger do you think there would be that most of the people of your country would lose their lives—a great deal, a fair amount, not very much, or none at all?*

The percentaged replies, grouped on a regional basis, are to be found in Table VII-3.

The similarities between the elite and public figures in each area are striking, indeed. Generalizing, the proportions thinking there would be "a greal deal" of danger that most of their populations would be wiped out came to seven out of ten of both types of combined samples in Canada, Mexico, and Brazil; a bit less than six out of ten in a collective sense for the four Western European countries; and approximately five out of ten among the Japanese.

These varying reactions possibly hinged in part on geographic proximity to the United States. The countries in the Americas were most fearful of devastation; the Europeans next; the far-away Japanese least of all.

Importance of NATO

Despite their relatively relaxed attitudes about the danger of war, at least at the abstract level, the Atlantic Alliance was considered important by respondents in the five member countries surveyed—that is, the Western Europeans and the Canadians. Responses to the following question indicate this point.

> QUESTION: *Now let's consider the North Atlantic Treaty Organiza-*
> *tion—NATO, that is. In terms of the best interest of*
> *this country, to what extent do you think it is*
> *important to preserve the unity and strength of the*
> *NATO Alliance—a great deal, a fair amount, not very*
> *much, or not at all?*

The results on this question were so varied that they are given in detail in Table VII-4.

To cast these figures on the importance of the unity and strength of NATO into more compact form, we shall resort once again to composite scores. In this

Table VII-3
Danger of Devastation from Nuclear War

	Western Europe		The Americas		Japan	
	Elites	Publics	Elites	Publics	Elite	Public
Great deal	58%	57%	70%	70%	50%	47%
Fair amount	27	25	19	17	33	35
Not very much	8	7	5	6	8	5
None at all	3	3	4	3	3	3
Don't know	4	8	2	4	6	10

Table VII-4
Importance of Unity and Strength of NATO

	Elites				
	British	French	German	Italian	Canadian
Great deal	70%	30%	56%	44%	52%
Fair amount	21	30	30	29	28
Not very much	6	19	7	12	11
Not at all	1	11	2	11	3
Don't know	2	10	5	4	6
	Publics				
Great deal	63	19	47	30	48
Fair amount	18	31	33	34	27
Not very much	4	11	10	7	8
Not at all	1	7	2	6	3
Don't know	14	32	8	23	14

case, "great deal" answers were rated at 100 points; "fair amount" at two-thirds of 100; "not very much" at one-third; and "not at all" at zero. The resultant ratings from the various samples are detailed below in the rank order of the combined averages:

	Elites	Publics	Combined Averages
British	88	89	89
German	82	79	81
Canadian	79	80	80
Italian	70	71	70
French	63	64	63
Overall Averages	76	77	77

Even the lowest of these scores (namely, 63 and 64 in the case of the French public and elite) were well above the median point of 50—in fact, just about up to the "fair amount" level. Far above these were scores around 70 in the case of the Italians, 80 among the Germans and Canadians, and close to 90 in Great Britain. Apparently, even in France the lessened threat of aggression has, as yet at least, not made our allies feel that the Atlantic Alliance is no longer needed.

Condition of NATO

Nevertheless, the pervasive view among all the elites (the publics were not asked this question) was that NATO is not in very good condition at the present time.

> QUESTION: *In terms of unity and strength, is it your impression that the condition of NATO at the present time is excellent, good, only fair, or poor?*

The replies are given in Table VII-5.

The composite scores for the various elites on this question (calculated with ratings ranging from 100 for "excellent" down to zero for "poor") reflect the preponderance of "only fair" answers in the table:

British	42
French	37
German	41
Italian	41
Canadian	43
Overall Average	41

It will be noted that every single one of these ratings is on the negative side, below the median point of 50; in fact, the uniformity among them is extraordinary. Thus the view among the elites of all five countries was clearly that the condition of NATO is not good, let alone excellent, but only fair.

Strengthening NATO

The preponderant feeling among the elites in Western Europe and Canada was, however, that the strength of NATO should only be kept at the present level, although significant proportions opted for an increase.

Table VII-5
Condition of NATO

	Elites				
	British	French	German	Italian	Canadian
Excellent	2%	3%	3%	3%	5%
Good	31	18	30	27	28
Only fair	54	52	44	50	47
Poor	10	14	16	11	11
Don't know	3	13	7	9	9

> QUESTION: *Do you think under present circumstances that the military strength of NATO should be increased, kept at the present level, reduced, or ended altogether?*

The replies are detailed in Table VII-6.

As can be seen, approximately one-half of elite respondents in Britain, Germany, and Canada chose the "present level" alternative, but if we add the "increased" percentages the totals come to very large majorities who favored either the present level or an increase: 87 percent in the case of the British, 84 percent of the Germans, and 71 percent of the Canadians.

In Italy and, especially, France, however, the picture was quite different. While modest pluralities did, indeed, favor maintaining the present level, in Italy the total of "reduced" or "ended altogether" responses came to 22 percent, as against 33 percent for "increased"; and in France to 25 percent, exactly the same as the "increased" figure. The only conclusion to be drawn is that in France the psychological underpinnings of the Atlantic Alliance are not solid and they are also fairly weak among the Italians.

Those members of the various elites who took the position that the strength of NATO should be increased were then asked this follow-up question:

> QUESTION: *Do you feel that your own country should contribute substantially more toward building up NATO's military strength, or not?*

Rather than totaling 100 percent, the figures in Table VII-7 add up, of course, only to the proportions which advocated beefing up the Alliance.

Overall, it will be seen that, while large majorities of those in favor of strengthening NATO were willing to contribute toward the cost, the across-the-board proportion favoring both increasing NATO's strength *and* contributing more toward that end still amounted to slightly less than one-fourth of all of those questioned. There were significantly lower figures in France and particularly Canada. In short, despite the perceived importance of NATO, cooperative

Table VII-6
Increasing or Reducing Strength of NATO

	Elites				
	British	French	German	Italian	Canadian
Increased	36%	25%	34%	33%	22%
Present level	51	39	50	39	49
Reduced	7	13	8	12	11
Ended altogether	3	12	2	10	6
Don't know	3	11	6	6	12

Table VII-7
Contributing to Strengthening NATO

	Elites				
	British	French	German	Italian	Canadian
Should	27%	21%	28%	24%	18%
Should not	8	3	4	8	3
Don't know	1	1	2	1	1
	36%	25%	34%	33%	22%

attitudes about beefing it up prevailed only among minorities of the elites in every one of the countries surveyed.

Withdrawal of U.S. Forces

Some respondents in Western Europe were considerably concerned about the prospect of weakened American military strength in Europe, but other elements joined the Canadians in not being particularly concerned. The responses listed in Table VII-8 were derived from the following question:

QUESTION: *How worried or concerned would you be if the United States substantially reduced the size of its own military forces now in Western Europe—a great deal, a fair amount, not very much, or not at all?*

Calculated in the way that has been familiar, the composite scores on this question looked like this:

	Elites	Publics	Combined Averages
British	67	67	67
German	68	63	65
Canadian	53	55	54
French	57	48	53
Italian	54	49	52
Overall Averages	60	56	58

Considering that the median point between relative concern and relative nonconcern is 50, it will be seen that only the British and the Germans were really disturbed about the prospect of reduced American military strength in

Europe. Very moderate degrees of concern were also registered by both Canadian samples and by the French and Italian elites. But the French and Italian publics appeared relatively apathetic about this issue. On an across-the-board basis, the overall averages of 56 for the publics and an even higher 60 for the elites showed overall concern but not in very great degree.

Against this background, and remembering that support for putting cash on the line to strengthen NATO directly was only in minority proportions, it is not surprising that as a whole the elites were completely stalemated on the issue of their countries contributing toward the retention of American forces in Europe at their present level.

> QUESTION: *The American Congress feels that the military forces the United States now has in Europe must be reduced if its NATO allies do not arrange to make up for more of the cost of keeping them there. Under these circumstances, do you think our government should take steps to help make up for more of these costs, or not?*

The results are given in Table VII-8.

It will be seen that the only real majority in favor of helping the United States support its contribution to NATO was to be found among the German elite. On the other hand, majorities of the Italians and Canadians were definitely opposed, with the British split 50-50 and the French sharply divided.

In short, it would appear that in general the Western Europeans and Canadians are all for NATO and believe in its importance, but not enough to make most of them eager to take on new financial burdens to strengthen it militarily, or to maintain the present level of America's contribution.

European Collective Defense

There was quite strong majority sentiment among the Western Europeans, however, in favor of collaborating toward the defense of Europe on a cooperative basis.

Table VII-8
Contributing Toward America's NATO Costs

	Elites					Overall Averages
	British	French	German	Italian	Canadian	
Should	47%	46%	59%	35%	36%	45%
Should not	47	40	29	58	53	45
Don't know	6	14	12	7	11	10

QUESTION: *Looking toward the future, do you think the major Western European nations, including (respondent's own country) should go further in developing their own strictly European collective defense arrangements, or not?*

The replies are presented in Table VII-9.

Majority support was strong among all groups, elite and public, except in the case of the French public. There the approval rating was 51 percent, with very few disagreeing but a very large "don't know."

The segment of each sample which said that Europe should go ahead developing its own collective defense was then asked the following question:

QUESTION: *Should such European collective defense arrangements be developed in association with the United States, or independently of the United States?*

The replies listed in Table VII-10 do not total 100 percent, but rather are the proportions of each sample which on the preceding question favored proceeding toward more collective defense arrangements.

As can readily be seen, majorities among those who thought European collective defense arrangements should be developed further felt this should be done in association with the United States in the case of both British and German samples, along with the Italian public. On the other hand, the French public opted predominantly for going ahead independently of the United States, with the French elite practically split down the middle. The Italian elite went along with the French public, preferring also by a relatively small margin independence from the United States in this regard.

Table VII-9
Undertaking Efforts to Develop Europe's Own Defense

| | Elites | | | | Overall Averages |
	British	French	German	Italian	
Should	72%	87%	71%	83%	78%
Should not	24	8	23	13	17
Don't know	4	5	6	4	5
				Publics	
Should	66	51	60	73	62
Should not	19	7	20	9	14
Don't know	15	42	20	18	24

Table VII-10
European Defense and the United States

	Elites				Overall Averages
	British	French	German	Italian	
European Defense Should Be Developed					
In association with the U.S.	48%	39%	47%	37%	43%
Independently of the U.S.	22	41	22	44	32
Don't know	2	7	2	2	3
	72%	87%	71%	83%	78%
			Publics		
In association with the U.S.	41	19	44	39	36
Independently of the U.S.	24	25	14	30	23
Don't know	1	7	2	4	3
	66%	51%	60%	73%	62%

As the overall averages show, however, the predominant feeling among the advocates of further European collective defense was that these moves should be made in association with the United States. However, the degree of sentiment for independence from the United States, amounting in the overall to almost one-third of the elite samples and one-quarter of the publics, may, indeed, be interpreted as a desire to get out from under dependence upon, if not dominance by the United States in defense matters.

Japan: Mutual Security Pact and Nuclear Weapons

The Japanese, and particularly the Japanese elite, were in favor of continuing their present security arrangements with America.

QUESTION: *In your opinion, should our Mutual Security Treaty with the United States be continued, or not?*

	Elite	Public
Should	68%	50%
Should not	14	21
Don't know	18	29

At the same time, the Japanese, and particularly the public, showed their customary aversion to nuclear weapons.

QUESTION: *Do you think that, to protect our own security and interest, Japan will eventually have to develop or acquire nuclear weapons, or not?*

	Elite	Public
Will have to	32%	20%
Will not have to	51	62
Don't know	17	18

The figures for the public on both of these questions show enormous differences from those obtained by the Institute for International Social Research on relatively similar questions in 1968. More particularly there has been a spectacular drop in the "don't knows" among the public, showing far less uncertainty today than existed at that time.

Defense Spending

There was relatively little sentiment among our samples in favor of their country increasing its spending for military purposes.

QUESTION: *Considering the situation at home and abroad, do you think the total amount your country is now spending for defense and military purposes should be increased, kept at the present level, reduced, or ended altogether?*

The composite scores on this question were calculated by weighting the "increase" answers at 100 points; "present level" at 50; and "reduced" or "ended altogether" at zero. Thus only scores above the median point of 50 indicate any degree of sentiment in favor of increased spending. The rating arranged in rank order of the combined averages are listed in Table VII-11.

The overall averages, all slightly below the median point of 50, demonstrate that prevailing sentiment was opposed to increases in defense spending but, by and large, in favor of maintaining approximately the present level. The only rating really leaning toward an increase was in the case of the Mexican public. On the other hand, the view that spending for military purposes should actually be decreased proved to be significantly prevalent among both public and elite samples in Italy and France, the Brazilian elite, and Japanese public.

Table VII-11
Spending on Defense
(Composite Scores)

	Elites	Publics	Combined Averages
Mexican	48	60	54
British	51	53	52
Canadian	49	56	52
German	51	46	49
Japanese	54	40	47
Brazilian	39	50	45
Italian	39	38	39
French	37	38	38
Overall Averages	46	48	47

It will be noted that there were very significant contrasts, cutting in both directions, between the views of the elites and the publics in Mexico, Canada, Japan, Brazil, and, to a lesser extent, Germany. In fact, greater discrepancies between the two types of samples emerged on this issue than on any other covered in our surveys. Nevertheless, since these variations tended to cancel each other out, the across-the-board overall averages for the elites and the publics turned out to be essentially similar.

Protection by the United States

No doubt, the main reason for lack of support for augmented defense expenditures is the general feeling of relaxation of international tensions, which has diminished any sense of imminent threats. However, a subsidiary factor may be that, with the limited exception of the Japanese, all of our samples had faith that the United States would come to their country's defense in the event of aggression, thus lessening their own need for augmented military power.

In the case of the Western European countries, the question in this regard was worded as follows:

> QUESTION: *Let's suppose that at some time in the future the Soviet Union launched an attack against Western Europe, involving your country, without attacking the United States directly. To what extent do you think you could rely on the United States to come to your defense with military force—a great deal, a fair amount, not very much, or not at all?*

In Japan the wording referred simply to the Soviets launching an attack against Japan. To increase plausibility, the references in Canada, Mexico, and Brazil were to the Soviets either launching or supporting such an attack.

Degrees of confidence in United States protection are indicated in Table VII-12. The composite scores, ranging from 100 for answers to the effect that respondents could rely on the United States "a great deal" to zero for "not at all," are arranged in the rank order of combined averages.

Incidentally, when the Japanese were asked to what extent they could rely on the United States to come to their defense with military force in the event of an attack by mainland China, the composite scores were exactly the same as those given above in the context of Soviet aggression.

In the face of much recent talk about Americans tending to return to isolationism or neo-isolationism, these scores, with the exception of the Japanese, are really extraordinary.

In fact, the astronomical ratings among the Canadians and Mexicans, who undoubtedly feel the United States would protect them in its own self-interest, and the British, who still apparently rely on the "special relationship" proved in World War II, are well-nigh incredible.

Without any question, except in the case of the Japanese, the results in the overall are an inspiring manifestation of trust and confidence in the fidelity of the United States of America as an ally and/or neighbor.

Table VII-12

Confidence in American Protection from Soviet Aggression
(Composite Scores)

	Elites	Publics	Combined Averages
Canadian	91	87	89
Mexican	85	74	80
British	79	80	80
Italian	78	73	76
Brazilian	77	73	75
French	73	71	72
German	69	66	67
Japanese	54	47	51
Combined Averages	76	71	74

VIII
Concerns, Aspirations, and Fears, Well-being

In this chapter we shall investigate the national needs, concerns, values, and preoccupations in the various countries surveyed to which America and Americans must tune in if we are to be respected, trusted, even appreciated.

Worries and Concerns

All our respondents were asked how worried or concerned they were about a long list of domestic and international problems. The only way to handle the flood of statistics that emerged is to reduce all of them to composite scores, in which, as usual, "a great deal" answers have been weighted at 100 points; "a fair amount" at two-thirds of 100; "not very much" at one-third; and "not at all" at zero. Thus any rating above the median point of 50 is indicative of at least a certain positive degree of concern, while any below 50 demonstrates relatively low concern. Across-the-board results for both public and elite samples in the eight countries surveyed as a whole are given in Table VIII-1 in the rank order of the combined averages (computed by adding the public and elite scores and dividing by two).

Domestic Problems

Obviously the six items of highest concern are all what used to be called "domestic." With the increasing interdependence that has developed in the world, however, a question of semantics now arises. Clearly the first four

Table VIII-1
Degrees of Worry and Concern
(Composite Scores)

		Elites	Publics	Combined Averages
1.	Rising prices and the cost of living	94	93	94
2.	Unemployment in respondent's own country	88	86	87
3.	Shortages or high prices of oil, gasoline, gas, coal, or electricity in respondent's own country	86	86	86
4.	Economic and business conditions generally	82	87	85
5.	Cleaning up waterways and reducing water pollution	83	85	84
6.	Reducing air pollution	82	85	83
7.	Maintaining respect for respondent's country in other countries	74	78	76
8.	Food shortages in various parts of the world	73	78	75
9.	Shortages or high prices of oil and other energy in the poorer countries of the world	71	76	74
10.	Maintaining close relations with the United States	65	71	68
11.	Respondent's country not developing fast enough in terms of industry and technology	65	68	67
12.	Keeping military and defense forces strong	66	62	64
13.	The future of the Middle East	56	70	63
14.	(NATO COUNTRIES ONLY) Keeping the military alliance with the United States strong	61	63	62
15.	The future of Western Europe	54	66	60
16.	Improving relations with the Soviet Union	56	62	59
17.	improving relations with mainland China	51	58	55
18.	The future of Indochina and Southeast Asia	45	56	50

subjects mentioned—inflation, unemployment, local energy shortages, and economic and business conditions—have all become increasingly affected by international economics. Similarly, in a good many situations the fifth and sixth items—reducing water and air pollution—also involve situations that extend outside the borders of one particular country. Perhaps, therefore, we must invent the designation "domestic-international" in speaking of most of these problems today.

On these top items of concern there were relatively few meaningful fluctuations in composite scores among the eight countries surveyed: the degree of concern was very high everywhere.

On the other hand, in the case of the only other "domestic" item, which was in eleventh place in the list—fear that respondent's country is not developing fast enough in terms of industry and technology—the number and degree of fluctuations were considerable. By far the highest combined averages for both samples were to be found in Britain (71), Italy (80), and Mexico (95), where industrial development has tended to lag or show signs of sluggishness. In sharp contrast, the combined average was only 17 in both Germany and Japan—that is to say, below the median point of 50, demonstrating no positive degree of concern whatever about this particular aspect of their economies.

International and Defense Issues

The first strictly "international" item emerged in seventh place in the list of concerns, with a combined average far below those on economic problems: namely, maintaining respect for respondent's country in other countries. This proved particularly important to the British, Italians, Canadians, and Mexicans, while the Japanese were not worried about it in any significant degree.

On the next item, in eighth place—food shortages in various parts of the world—the Germans and Japanese showed less "compassion" than respondents in the other countries surveyed.

Turning to the twelfth item—keeping military and defense forces strong—the rather surprising fact emerged that those most concerned were the British (combined average for both samples, 77). On the other hand, the lowest similar average for both samples was to be found in France (57), with ratings very nearly down to the median point of 50 emerging in the case of both the German and Japanese publics (53 and 52, respectively).

Among all the items having to do with particular nations or regions of the world, the leading one, ranking tenth in the list, had to do with maintaining close relations with the United States, which drew a by no means low combined average for all samples of 68. Variations in country scores on this subject were considerable. The highest combined averages emerged in Britain (75), Canada (80), and Mexico (78). Somewhat lower than average combined ratings were given in Japan (64) and especially Brazil (60) and France (59).

On a more restricted basis, wide variations also emerged when the issue posed in the four Western European Countries and Canada was that of keeping the NATO alliance with the United States strong. The combined averages for both samples, which in the overall came to 62, ranged downward as follows: Britain 76, Canada 69, Germany 60, Italy 57, and France 49—a rating showing no positive degree of concern at all about alliance with the United States.

Somewhat surprisingly, in view of the dependency especially of Western Europe and Japan on Middle Eastern oil, concern about the future of the Middle East came in only in thirteenth place. There was even less overall worry about the future of Western Europe, largely because of a general lack of apprehension in the three countries in the Americas and Japan, unlike those in Europe itself.

Similarly, concern about improving relations with the Soviet Union and

China, respectively, was not very great (combined averages 59 and 55, respectively). The highest scores in both respects emerged in Britain and Canada; the lowest in Italy and Brazil. The Japanese were a bit below average in regard to improving relations with the Soviet Union (55) but, along with Canada, far above average on the related question regarding relations with China (both combined averages were 65).

Minimal concern (actually below the median point of 50 in the case of the combined publics) was exhibited in regard to the future of Indochina and Southeast Asia. This was true even among the Japanese, who one might assume would be most interested in that part of the world (combined average for both samples was 53). Apparently most of our samples would be happy if that particular part of the world and its problems would just quietly slide into oblivion.

In sum total, however, it is clear that economic and pollution problems loomed much larger in the concerns of all samples than any others our respondents were asked about.

National Aspirations and Fears

As stated above, the listing of relative degrees of concern about the wide range of subjects discussed above gave us a picture of what elites and publics in the countries surveyed were worrying about on a very broad, systematically sketched canvas. In our surveys, however, we were also interested in finding out what was really in the forefront of respondents' minds in the way of personally felt preoccupations about national problems as they went routinely about their daily lives.

To accomplish this, we asked them early in the interviews, without previous reminders or any prompting, to express in their own words what aspirations were embodied in their own concept of the best possible situation for their nation, and what worries and fears were embodied in their idea of the worst possible national situation. The first of the two questions along this line was worded as follows:

> QUESTION: *What are your wishes and hopes for the future of (respondent's) country? If you picture the future of this country in the best possible light, how would things look, let us say, about ten years from now? Take your time in answering; such things aren't easy to express.*

The most significant national aspirations mentioned voluntarily by respondents in the four countries surveyed in Western Europe, the three in the Americas, and Japan are listed in Table VIII-2.

Table VIII-2
National Aspirations

	Western Europe		The Americas		Japan	
	Elites	Publics	Elites	Publics	Elite	Public
Political						
Good government: honest, efficient, balanced	21%	13%	10%	9%	2%	5%
Democratic of representative government	10	4	3	2	2	2
National unity; political stability	15	10	11	12	4	3
Economic						
Improved or decent standard of living	28	29	46	41	14	12
Economic stability; no inflation	33	29	17	22	10	8
Employment	16	27	11	16	22	21
Social						
Social justice; greater equality; elimination of discrimination based on class or economic status	23	20	14	9	2	3
Adequate social security	6	8	3	4	10	11
International						
Peace	11	12	5	6	6	7
Lessening of tensions, disarmament; better relations with Communist bloc	6	3	*	*	2	1
Enhanced status or importance; greater leadership role; be militarily strong	10	6	10	7	4	3
National independence	6	4	14	11	*	1

An inspection of Table VIII-2 makes it obvious, as was the case in the systematic listing of concerns, that economic matters strongly dominated the national aspirations respondents had in the forefront of their minds: standard of living, employment, economic stability, and control of inflation. The combined standard of living figures were greater in the Americas than in Europe because of amazingly high mentions of this subject by both Mexican samples. Preoccupations with economic stability, on the other hand, were well above average in France, Germany, and Canada. The lower than average level of concern about this subject in Britain and Italy is difficult to understand in view of the problems which have been facing those countries in connection with economic stability.

References to political subjects in general were comparatively low, and where the figures for a region as a whole were relatively higher there were local focuses to explain this. For example the greater than average level of mentions of good government and democratic or representative government among the combined Western Europe elites was due to an unusually high degree of concern about these matters among elite Italians.

Similarly, preoccupation with the problem of national unity and political stability was extremely low in Japan but much greater in the combined European figures because of higher than average mentions by both samples in France, where anything approaching a real national consensus has been lacking during the post-de Gaulle years, and in the Americas because of the Canadians, who were obviously worried about the British-French split in their national population.

Considerations of social justice also rated extremely low in Japan, but high in Western Europe chiefly because this appeared to be an issue of really burning concern among the French.

In the case of international matters, references to peace and the lessening of international tensions were markedly lower than in the past. Relatively little interest was displayed in enhancing national status or playing more of a leadership role in Italy, Germany, and Japan, despite the fact that the latter two have the greatest potential in these respects of any of the countries surveyed. Preoccupations with these matters were greater, although still not high in Britain, France, Canada, and Brazil. Higher than average mentions of national independence in the Americas were due almost entirely to the Canadians, who were obviously apprehensive about U.S. dominance.

The companion query to the question regarding national aspirations and fears was worded this way:

QUESTION: *Taking the other side of the picture, what are your fears and worries for the future of (respondent's country)? If you picture the future of your country in the worst possible light, how would things look about ten years from now?*

In this case the most meaningful mentions of worries and fears by respondents are listed, again on a regional basis, in Table VIII-3.

As would be expected, the patterning of the results on national worries and fears tended to be similar to that on wishes and hopes. The concentration again was on the economic side: inadequate standard of living, economic instability, and unemployment. This ties in, of course, with the finding mentioned in Chapter IV that, when elite respondents were asked what United States policies and actions would be in their own national interests, they placed the chief emphasis on economics: improving the world economy and bettering economic relations with their own country or region.

Japanese fears having to do with standard of living were especially high for a particular reason: far more of them than of other samples were afraid, not that their standard of living would fail to improve, but that it would actually deteriorate, in view, no doubt, of the enormous difficulties facing their national economy because of world economic factors. Fear of unemployment was

Table VIII-3
National Worries and Fears

	Western Europe		The Americas		Japan	
	Elites	Publics	Elites	Publics	Elite	Public
Political						
Bad government: dishonest, inefficient	7%	5%	7%	6%	3%	2%
Communism	12	8	6	3	5	3
No democracy or representative government	16	7	4	1	1	3
Lack or loss of freedom	8	4	3	2	1	*
Lack of law and order	9	10	6	6	2	7
Disunity; political instability	21	19	20	16	4	4
Economic						
No improvement in, or inadequate standard of living; failure to preserve present standard of living	21	20	15	12	41	34
Economic instability, inflation, recession	32	27	20	26	4	2
Unemployment	21	29	10	11	20	18
Social						
Abuses of labor: strikes, labor unrest	10	9	3	2	1	*
Unlimited population growth	3	5	8	8	7	4
International						
War	7	10	9	16	12	7
Loss of status or importance; failure to exert leadership	5	2	*	*	*	*
Loss of national independence	7	5	12	7	*	*
Threat or aggression from a foreign power	6	3	2	3	2	1

significantly higher among the French and Germans than in Great Britain and Italy, where the general economic situation is much worse.

On the political side, mentions of bad government were at low ebb, and fear of communism was muted except to a limited extent in Western Europe. Concern about the loss of democracy or representative government was unusually high among the Italians. References to the lack of law and order were significantly few compared to what would have emerged on this subject in the United States.

"Disunity; political instability" was a matter of little concern among the Japanese but, as in the case of aspirations, loomed much larger than average in France and Canada, no doubt for the reasons mentioned above. The figures in this respect were also higher than average in Mexico.

Under the "social" category, "abuses of labor: strikes, labor unrest" was a subject of considerable preoccupation to the British and the French but not elsewhere. Unlimited population growth received very few mentions—a fact which will be brought up again in the following section.

As in the case of aspirations for peace, the fear of war was mentioned by amazingly low proportions of respondents. In fact, references to peace as an aspiration and war as a fear were at the lowest ebb ever recorded in opinion surveys the Institute for International Social Research has conducted in all parts of the world over the past twenty years. Mentions of threats or aggression from a foreign power were also minimal. Clearly, there is very little sense of international danger at this stage.

A decline in status or failure to exert leadership once again showed up as of minor concern, and the figures on loss of national independence were as high as they were only because of the Canadians, as we found to be the case in discussing national aspirations.

In short, on the whole our samples were not really worried very much about anything as they went about their daily lives except the economic problems of unemployment, standard of living, and economic instability or inflation. At this stage, these have clearly stolen the show even from such dazzling matters as war and peace, not to mention more mundane problems of domestic policy.

Economic and Population Growth

The item discussed in the systematic list of concerns about respondent's country not progressing fast enough industrially and technologically, plus the limited mentions referred to above of unlimited population growth as a national fear led us to introduce a new subject at this point: the issue of regulating population and/or economic growth. The question on the first of these subjects was worded as follows:

> QUESTION: *Do you think that population growth throughout the world will have to be brought under control to avoid serious shortages of water, land, food, and other national resources, or not?*

The answers were overwhelmingly affirmative, ranging from 64 percent who said regulation of world population would be necessary among the Japanese public to 92 percent of the Mexican public, with huge majorities in the case of all the other elites and publics falling in between.

Yet when respondents had been asked the following question earlier in the interview, an entirely converse result emerged:

QUESTION: *Over the coming·years, would you like to see the population of your own country grow substantially, grow moderately, stay at about the present level, or decrease?*

In not a single sample surveyed did a preponderant opinion emerge that a limitation of population should be extended to their own country. In fact, excluding the French public, where the proportion was only a plurality, the majorities listed below favored at least a moderate increase:

	Elites	Publics
Canada	74%	63%
Brazil	68	71
Germany	68	50
Mexico	51	53
France	52	43

In the remaining three countries, where the results were more complicated, we shall give the figures in detail, combining the "grow substantially" and "grow moderately" categories to make perceptions easier.

	Britain		Italy		Japan	
	Elite	Public	Elite	Public	Elite	Public
National population should:						
Grow	12%	17%	18%	29%	28%	18%
Stay at present level	54	51	44	45	49	55
Decrease	33	31	38	23	20	23
Don't know	1	1	*	3	3	4

Thus even in these three divergent countries preponderant opinion was in favor of maintaining the present level, with substantial minorities opting for "decrease" only among both British samples and the Italian elite.

Much the same kind of divorcement occurred on the subject of regulating economic growth. It will be recalled that, in discussing the systematic list of concerns at the beginning of this chapter, "fear that respondent's country is not developing fast enough in terms of industry and technology" was high only in Britain, Italy, and Mexico, where problems have been experienced along this line.

On the other hand, concern was low in France and Canada, where the rate of development has obviously been satisfactory, and very low, indeed, in Germany and Japan, where growth has been spectacular. The implication clearly is that industrial and technological growth at the national level was considered a desideratum by all concerned. Yet when the following question changed the context to a world basis, the views that emerged were very different:

> QUESTION: *And do you think that worldwide economic growth will have to be brought under control to avoid such shortages, or not?*

As in the case of population growth, approval of regulation of global economic growth tended to be widespread. The Japanese were the exception to a limited extent; but even among them a plurality of 46 percent of the public and majority of 52 percent of the elite were in favor. In the case of all other samples, however, the majorities opting for regulation ranged from 60 percent of the Canadian elite to 89 percent of both the French public and elite.

In short, in the case of both population and economic growth, the feeling is that "they" should be regulated but not "us." Undoubtedly, this kind of psychological bifurcation will increasingly complicate steps to handle global problems which are becoming ever more complicated in demanding widespread if not universal national cooperation.

National Well-being

After respondents had sketched their own concepts of the best and the worst possible situations for their country through detailing their national wishes and hopes and worries and fears, respectively, they were handed a picture of a ladder with steps numbered from ten at the top to zero at the bottom, and given these directions:

> QUESTION: *Let's suppose the top of the ladder represents the very best possible situation for (respondent's country); the bottom, the very worst possible situation for this country. Please show me on which step of the ladder you think (respondent's country) is at the present time. On which step would you say this country was about five years ago? If things go more or less as you expect, where would you guess (respondent's country) will be on the ladder about five years from now?*

Under this scheme the highest possible rating would be 10.0; the lowest 0.0. The average ladder ratings, past, present, and future, that emerged from our various samples are given in Table VIII-4, ranked in the order of scores for the present indicating degrees of relative national well-being.

In analyzing shifts in ratings from past to present and from present to future we must bear in mind what was brought out in Chapter VI on "Power and Importance": namely, that a change is not significant statistically unless it amounts to at least 0.6 steps of the ladder.

Taking this into account, it is apparent from Table VIII-4 that, while the Canadians and Germans had the greatest sense of current national well-being among our samples as a whole, they had no feelings of progress over the past five

Table VIII-4
Average National Ladder Ratings

	Past	Present	Future	Shift: Past to Present	Shift: Present to Future
Canada					
Elite	6.4	6.6	6.7	+0.2	+0.1
Public	6.5	6.6	6.4	+0.1	−0.2
Germany					
Elite	6.6	6.5	6.3	−0.1	−0.2
Public	6.5	6.1	6.0	−0.4	−0.1
Brazil					
Elite	4.2	5.7	7.5	+1.5	+1.8
Public	3.8	6.0	7.7	+2.2	+1.7
Japan					
Elite	6.1	5.9	6.0	−0.2	+0.1
Public	5.9	5.4	5.5	−0.5	+0.1
Mexico					
Elite	5.0	5.2	6.4	+0.2	+1.2
Public	5.2	5.6	6.4	+0.4	+0.8
France					
Elite	5.8	5.3	5.5	−0.5	+0.2
Public	6.0	5.1	5.3	−0.9	+0.2
Britain					
Elite	6.2	4.6	4.6	−1.6	±0.0
Public	6.5	4.4	5.0	−2.1	+0.6
Italy					
Elite	5.7	3.2	3.7	−2.5	+0.5
Public	5.7	3.6	4.3	−2.1	+0.7

years, and were not optimistic about improvement in their national situation over the next five years.

In these two respects the Brazilians were unique. They felt quite well off in the present, and exhibited an enormous sense both of progress and of optimism. The Mexicans went half way along these lines: they thought their country had not progressed over the last five years, but were significantly hopeful that there would be amelioration of their national lot in the future.

The Japanese showed neither a statistically significant sense of change from past to present nor from present to future. The same was true of the French, except that the French public sensed meaningful deterioration from past to present.

The lowest scores of all on current national well-being were to be found among the British and Italians. On top of this, both samples in each of these countries saw dramatic deterioration in their national situation from past to present, and, while the publics thought there would be slight, but significant improvement in the future, the elites did not.

In short, comparing the results from all samples—except the Brazilians and to a lesser extent the Mexicans—with the strong sense of progress and hopefulness that has customarily emerged when the Institute for International Social Research administered this so-called Self-Anchoring Striving Scale in past years, one can only say that the picture that has evolved is anything but buoyant. This is an indication, no doubt, of our respondents' awareness and concern about the deeply serious problems confronting them in today's increasingly complicated and interrelated world.

# IX Chapter-by-Chapter Summary

In conclusion, we shall give a chapter-by-chapter summary of the major findings discussed in detail above, in the hope of finally pulling results a little more together.

1. International Cooperation and Orientations

When asked with which nations and international organizations their own country should cooperate very closely, it turned out that, apart from the United Nations, the Canadians focused primarily on Western Europe and the United States, but also gave attention very broadly to all other parts of the world.

Japanese orientations were much more severely restricted primarily, along with the United Nations, to America and mainland China, with very little concern for other Asian countries or regional organizations.

In contrast, in addition to the United Nations, the primary concentration of the Mexicans and Brazilians was on their own region of Latin America, with the United States distinctly subordinated.

Similarly, the British, French, Germans, and Italians as a group placed primary importance on the European Economic Community and countries in Western Europe, with the United States and NATO in second place, and the United Nations third. In fact, if faced with a choice between closer relations with other Western European countries or America, all samples with the exception of the British public, but including the British elite, indicated they would choose their neighbors rather than their more distant cousin.

On a comparative basis, the Canadians were way out front in number of references to close cooperation with the United States and NATO. Not too far behind came the Germans, with the British in third place. The Italians came in a not very impressive fourth, with the French far in the rear. In the other three countries surveyed (where mentions of NATO were inappropriate because they were not members), the Japanese and Mexicans seemed to have close cooperation with America on their minds with about the same intensity as the Italians, while the Brazilians exhibited about as low a degree of concern in this respect as did the French.

2. The European Economic Community

There was a virtual standoff in the Western European countries surveyed as to whether the basic interests of the United States and those of the Common Market countries are "fairly well in agreement" or "rather different," with the French particularly thinking they are different and the Italians believing in above average proportions that they are compatible.

As to relations between America and the Common Market countries, plurality sentiment by a small margin was in favor of closer ties. The Italians and particularly the British were preponderantly of this opinion, but the French thought the current degree of intimacy is already "about right." The Germans were almost evenly divided on this issue. Again with considerable variations, the preponderant guess was that, in the future, relations between the Common Market and America would, in fact, remain about as they now are, rather than becoming closer.

The Western Europeans tended to feel that their basic interests and Japan's are "rather different," and the predominant belief was that current relationships are "about right," although a substantial proportion thought they are "not close enough." The Japanese agreed that there is no very positive mutuality of interests but a sizable majority, nevertheless, wanted closer ties with the Common Market.

Majorities of the Canadian samples believed their basic interests and those of the EEC are at least "fairly well in agreement" and that their relationships should become closer.

The British, French, Germans, and Italians felt that the basic interests of the various members of the EEC as a whole are only slightly in agreement at the present time. Nevertheless, there was very strong sentiment, even among the British, to the effect that continuing participation in the Common Market would be beneficial to their respective countries. In fact, all of them, including the British, favored by large majorities further steps to integrate Western Europe. With the British opposed, a plurality of the French public and large majorities of all the other samples would be willing to go so far as creating a political federation of Western Europe with a central government having the final authority.

3. General Attitudes Toward the United States
and American Corporations

USIA data show that, in general, attitudes towards the United States were high
between 1961 and 1965, very low during 1967 and 1968, and mixed (some high,
some low) from 1969 to 1972. Our current surveys show that mixed evaluations
continued to prevail at the end of 1974.

To start with, except for the Italian public, at the abstract level, opinions of
"the United States, its policies, and actions" at the time of our surveys were
unfavorable in the case of all samples, elites and publics, and especially adverse
among the French, Japanese, and to a slightly lesser extent the Canadians.

In terms of the image of the United States, there was a virtual stalemate
between positive and negative factors, although the total picture was greatly
improved compared to highly adverse results obtained in most of the countries
covered in 1968.

Nevertheless, except among the French, feelings about mutuality of interests
with America, which are far more important in influencing national policies and
behavior than mere "popularity," were definitely positive in all the countries
surveyed, and especially so in Britain, Italy, Germany, and Canada. In line with
this, preponderant sentiment was to the effect that it would be beneficial to the
countries concerned to cooperate with the United States in dealing with world
scarcities and high prices of oil and other raw materials.

The predominant view in the case of every sample was that current closeness
of relations with the United States is "about right," although substantial
minorities of both samples among the Mexicans, Brazilians, Japanese, and the
Italian elite felt that their country's ties with America are already "too close."
Looking to the future, most samples saw their relationship with America
remaining "about the same," but preponderantly both samples in Mexico and
the public samples in Italy and Brazil saw ties becoming closer, contrary to their
wishes.

The views of the Canadian and French publics were that the operations of
American businesses and industries within their own countries are harmful. The
Canadian elite, however, along with both samples in Japan and Germany, tended
to straddle the fence on this issue. Somewhat surprisingly, however, the
prevailing opinion among the British, Brazilians, Mexicans and Italians was that
American corporations are positively beneficial to their own national interests.

4. America's International Role, Objectives,
and Leadership

In an across-the-board sense, there was a complete stalemate between positive
and negative views as to "the role the United States is playing in international
affairs and on the world scene generally at the present time." Both British

samples and the Italian public tended to be favorable; the Mexicans tended toward the unfavorable side, and the ratings among the Japanese and French were definitely adverse. The results from the rest of the samples were, in effect, neutral.

Nevertheless, on a question asking whether the United States is genuinely concerned about the welfare of other nations or only about advancing its own interests in the world, preponderant views were comfortably generous. Majorities in most countries of both publics and to an even greater extent elites felt that America is motivated by the good of the world or by a combination of this and the advancement of its own interests. Only in Mexico and Brazil did majorities point solely to the entirely selfish goal of advancing American interests.

It was the belief of the elites that the principal objectives or goals the United States is trying to attain at present are clustered around maintaining or increasing its own power (political, economic, military, and in general), plus seeking world peace and the reduction of tensions.

Asked to what extent the United States really tries to understand and take into account their own country's best interests, the replies from the French samples were highly adverse, with the Japanese and Canadians, along with the Brazilian elite, less so. But both samples of the Germans, British, and Mexicans, plus the Italian public, gave preponderantly favorable replies.

The kinds of American policies and actions elite respondents felt would be in the best interests of their own countries were varied but tended to cluster especially around economic matters: improving the world economic and monetary situation, on the one hand, and bettering economic relations with their own countries or regions, on the other.

Majority sentiment among both elites and publics was to the effect that, at the present time, relations between the United States and the Soviet Union are not excellent nor good, but "only fair," showing that the bulk of respondents do not consider "detente" something to be heavily relied on, as yet at least. But all concerned saw future relations as either remaining about the same or improving, so clearly did not expect any crunch between the two superpowers over the next few years. Along this line, only the French and Mexicans believed there was any significant danger the United States would sell out its allies or neighbors to bring off better deals with the Soviets.

Asked how much confidence they had in the ability of the United States to provide wise leadership in dealing with world problems, the ratings were remarkably favorable in Mexico, Germany, and Great Britain; moderately so in Italy, Canada, and among the Japanese elite; and adverse only in Brazil and France.

The tendency everywhere was for the elites to feel that the United States will go on playing a vigorous role on the international front, rather than reverting to some kind of isolationism. With the exception of the French and the Mexicans, all other elites applauded this.

Asked whether they would like to see the influence of the United States in their own parts of the world increase, decrease, or remain at the present level, in the Americas the elites in Canada, Mexico, and especially Brazil opted for a weakened role, with the publics in those countries splintered on this issue. In Western Europe, the Italian elite preponderantly wanted the influence of the United States to decrease, and the French elite was split almost evenly between "decrease" and "present level." However, the predominant opinion among all the other European samples was that American influence should remain at about the present level. The Japanese agreed, but with less conviction, about U.S. influence in Asia.

5. Attitudes Toward the Soviet Union and China

Opinions of the Soviet Union, its policies, and actions were decidedly adverse in all the countries surveyed—far more so than opinions of the United States. The overall averages in the case of mainland China were also on the negative side but to a much lesser extent. In fact China nosed out the United States among the combined elites and equaled the United States in the case of the publics. The general conclusion is that none of these three powers can be considered popular in any affirmative way.

Feelings of mutuality of interests with the Soviet Union were also conspicuously lacking. The Japanese (the only country in which the issue was raised) also felt that their interests and those of China were either "rather" different" or "very different." In both respects, the United States came out far ahead in all countries surveyed.

Nevertheless, huge majorities of both the Japanese elite and public were in favor of closer relations with China. On an across-the-board basis the combined elites in the other countries leaned toward the view that current relations with China are "not close enough," while the publics tended more to think such relations are already "about right."

In the related question about the Soviet Union, while the feeling that relations with the USSR are not close enough proved to be very considerable, the predominant preference in all countries but one tended to be that the present situation is "about right." The exception was the Japanese, a sizable majority of whom wanted more intimate ties with the Soviet Union.

In contrast, there was a considerable reaching out, particularly among the elites, for closer relations with the Eastern European nations other than the Soviet Union.

Confidence in the ability of the Soviet Union to provide wise leadership in dealing with world problems was very decidedly wanting among both elites and publics, and the scores in the case of confidence in the Chinese were even more adverse—in both cases vastly below the affirmative ratings given the United States in this regard.

6. Power and Importance

Asked to rate various nations in terms of power and importance, the various respondents saw no meaningful upward shift in the standing of the United States either from ten years ago to the present, nor from the present to ten years from now. In contrast, the present rating assigned the Soviet Union was very much higher than the past, but few of the samples expected the Russians to enhance their position significantly further over the next ten years.

Both samples in Italy, Mexico, Brazil, and Japan, plus the French elite thought the United States was still ahead of the USSR at present; but both samples in Britain, Germany, and Canada, joined by the French public, felt that a state of equivalence has already been achieved by the Soviets. Furthermore, except for the Brazilian public, all concerned prophesized equality by ten years from now, if not already today.

This prospect proved to be a welcome one, however, since a preponderance of all samples except the British public thought it preferable for America and the Soviet Union to be about equal in power, rather than for the United States to maintain superiority.

The present power and importance ratings assigned mainland China, Japan, and the Common Market countries as a whole were all about the same and much lower than those of the United States or the Soviet Union. It was anticipated that all would increase in power and influence over the next ten years. Nevertheless, it was expected that all of the three, notably including China, while constituting about mutually equal significant power centers, would nevertheless remain significantly below the two superpowers.

In rating the power and importance of their own countries, the British and Italians saw a major drop over the past ten years and, although expecting some improvement in the future, did not think that ten years from now they would even be up to where they had been ten years ago. The French saw no substantial increment in their own power and influence. However, all the other samples envisioned substantial, and in some cases gigantic enhancements in their country's relative standing. Nevertheless, none of them, either as of the present or the future, placed themselves in a position even remotely approaching that of America or the Soviet Union.

In general, all the samples surveyed wanted their country to gain more power and importance in the world by playing a more active role and taking on more responsibilities. Some hesitation on this score was expressed by the Japanese public, however, and a great deal by both samples in Germany.

7. War, Alliances, Defense

With the somewhat puzzling exception of the Brazilians and Mexicans, who perceived considerable danger, the rest of our samples had relatively little fear that a war would break out within the next ten years that would bring sorrow or suffering to their own country.

There was even less belief in the likelihood of a nuclear war between the United States and the Soviet Union. However, all samples without exception thought that, if such a nuclear confrontation did occur, the lives of most of the people in their respective countries would be at stake. Variations in the degree of reactions seemed to hinge on geographic proximity to the United States: the countries in the Americas were the most fearful of such devastation; the Western Europeans next; the far-away Japanese least of all.

All samples in the member states of the Atlantic Alliance expressed the belief that it is important to their own countries to preserve the unity and strength of NATO. The elites in both Western Europe and Canada believed, however, that the condition of NATO at the present time is not good, let alone excellent, but only fair.

Nevertheless, the prevailing opinion was that the military strength of NATO should simply be kept at the present level, although sizable minorities in most countries opted for an increase. In contrast, significant minority proportions of the Italian and especially French elites were in favor of actually decreasing NATO's clout, or even ending the arrangement altogether.

Most of those who favored beefing up NATO were willing for their own countries to contribute to the cost; but the proportions approving both increasing NATO's strength and contributing to the cost came to less than one-quarter of the total elite samples in the NATO countries surveyed.

Only the British and German elites were really disturbed about the prospects of a reduction in the strength of American forces in Europe. Both Canadian samples, along with the French and Italian elites, registered only very moderate concern, while the French and Italian publics appeared largely apathetic about this issue. When it came to the question, posed only to the NATO members' elites, of their respective countries making up more of the costs in order to keep the level of American forces in Europe up to par, the only real real majority in favor was to be found among the Germans. Majorities of the Italians and Canadians were definitely opposed, with the British splitting 50-50, and the French sharply divided.

In short, while the Western Europeans and Canadians said they were in favor of NATO and believed in its importance, this feeling was not strong enough to make them eager to take on new financial burdens either to strengthen NATO in a direct sense, or to maintain the present level of the U.S. contribution.

Except among the French public, majority support was strong in the case of all elite and public samples in Western Europe to go further in developing strictly European collective defense arrangements. In the case of both samples in Britain and Germany, along with the Italian public, majorities among those who felt this way believed it should be done in association with the United States. On the other hand, the Italian elite and French public opted predominantly for going ahead independently of the United States, with the French elite practically split down the middle. Nevertheless the predominant general feeling among the advocates of further European collective defense arrangements was that these moves should be made in association with America.

A majority of the public and especially the elite in Japan was in favor of continuing the Mutual Security Pact with the United States. Also, majorities, especially high in the case of the public, opposed Japan developing or acquiring nuclear weapons.

On defense spending as a whole, the prevailing sentiment in general was in favor of maintaining the present level and opposed to increases, except in the case of the Mexican public which opted for a stronger military. The view that such expenditures should actually be decreased proved to be preponderant, however, among both public and elite samples in Italy and France, the Brazilian elite, and the Japanese public.

With the exception of the Japanese, who were lukewarm on the subject, an amazingly high proportion of all samples felt they could rely on the United States to come to their defense with military force in the event of aggression by the Soviets. This was true even of the French, despite the fact that their country had long since withdrawn from NATO's integrated military-command structure and expelled its headquarters. The astronomical confidence displayed on this issue by the Canadians, Mexicans, and British was well-high incredible at a time when talk about Americans reverting in some degree to isolationism is having a good deal of currency.

8. Concerns, Aspirations, Fears, and Well-being

When asked systematically about how worried and concerned they were about a long list of problems, respondents everywhere placed the main emphasis upon economic ones: inflation, unemployment, energy shortages, and economic and business conditions generally. Next in order came concern about reducing both water and air pollution.

Among the several international items, the highest ratings were given to maintaining respect for one's own country abroad, food and oil shortages or high prices in various parts of the world, and maintaining close relations with the United States. The lowest scores of all were in connection with improving relations with the Soviet Union and China, and particularly concern about the future of Indochina and Southeast Asia.

When asked about the wishes and hopes embodied in their own concepts of the best possible situation for their country, and the worries and fears illustrative of the worse possible situation, the emphases again were placed on economics: standard of living, employment, economic stability and control of inflation. References to political and social matters tended to be low, except that disunity and political instability were of particular concern to the French and Canadians.

Mentions of peace as a national aspiration and war as a fear were at the lowest ebb ever recorded in the surveys the Institute for International Social Research has conducted in all parts of the world over the last twenty years.

Our respondents tended to be overwhelmingly aware of the need to regulate both population and economic growth on a worldwide basis, but were generally opposed to making such limitations in their own countries.

In terms of national well-being, the Canadians and Germans felt their respective countries to be the best off, and the British and Italians the worst off. Furthermore, the latter two have had a sense of severe national deterioration over the preceding five years. The Brazilians, in contrast, exhibited strong feelings both of progress and of optimism, and were joined in being optimistic by the Mexicans. In sum, however, with the Brazilians and to a lesser extent the Mexicans excepted, the mood that has emerged from these surveys tends to be gloomy, especially when compared to the bouncy sense of national progress and the feelings of optimism that have customarily emerged from most similar studies in recent years.

This reflects, no doubt, an acute awareness of the vast problems confronting the world and all of its nations at the present time.

Index

Africa, 2, 6
Americas, the: and communist countries, 60; domestic concerns of, 93, 94; and US, 54, 105; and war danger, 78, 107
Arab countries, 7, 8. *See also* Middle East
Asia, xxvi, 2; 4-5, 6, 54, 92, 101, 105
Atlantic Alliance. *See* North Atlantic Treaty Organization
Australia, 8

Benelux countries, 9
Brazil, xxvii; attitude toward communist countries, 57, 59, 60, 61, 62, 92; attitude toward US, 5-6, 10, 30, 32, 33, 34, 35, 37, 91, 102, 103; international orientation of, xxv, 5-7, 10, 101, 102; national concerns of, 91, 92, 94, 100, 109; and US role, 40, 41, 44, 45, 47, 51, 53, 54, 104, 105; and US-USSR power balance, 67, 68, 69, 70, 106; and war danger, 75, 77, 78, 86, 87, 88, 106-107, 108; as world power, xxvi, 72
Burns, Robert, xxvii

Canada, xxvi, 7, 8, 72; attitude toward communist countries, 57, 59, 61, 62, 92; attitude toward US, 25, 30, 33, 37, 91, 103; and EEC, 18-19, 102; international orientation of, 2, 10, 101-102; and NATO, 2, 10, 78, 79, 80, 81, 82, 83, 91, 101-102, 107; national concerns of, 91, 92, 93, 94, 95, 96, 97-98, 99, 108, 109; and US role, 40, 44, 45, 47, 51, 53, 54, 104, 105; and US-USSR power balance, 67, 68, 106; and war danger, 76, 78, 87, 88, 108
China, 4, 5, 46, 70, 101; attitudes toward, 55-56, 58-60, 91-92, 105, 108; as world power, xxvi, 63, 70-72, 105, 106
Cofremca (France), xxvi
Commission on Critical Choices for Americans, ix-x, xvii, xxvii; members, xi-xvi

Common Market. *See* European Economic Community
Crespi, Leo, 23n
Cuba, 7

Defense spending, 86-87, 108
De Gaulle, Charles, 22
Doxa (Italy), xxvi

EEC. *See* European Economic Community
East Germany, 61
Eastern Europe, 2, 7, 61-62, 105
Economic stability, 89-91, 92, 93, 94-95, 96, 104, 108; and population growth, 96-98, 109
Elite vs. public opinion, xxvii; attitudes toward US, 27-30, 32-33; British, xxv-xxvi; and defense spending, 87; and NATO, 80-82, 107; and US role, 41-42, 104; and US-USSR power balance, 66-68
Emnid-Institut (West Germany), xxvi
European Economic Community, xxv, 7, 8, 9, 13-22, 101, 102; and Canada, 18-19, 102; and Great Britain, 20-21; and Japan, 17-18, 102; mutual interests, 19-22; and US, 13-17, 102; and unification of Europe, 21-22; as world power, xxvi, 70-74, 106

France, 8, 65; attitude toward communist countries, 55, 59, 61, 62; attitude toward US, 11, 16, 25, 26-27, 30, 31, 32, 33, 37, 103; and EEC, 9, 14-15, 16, 19, 101, 102; international orientation of, 9, 10, 11, 101, 102; and NATO, xxvi, 10, 79, 81, 83, 91, 101, 102, 107, 108; national concerns of, 91, 93, 94, 95, 96, 97-98, 100; and US role, xxvi, 10, 40, 44, 45, 51, 52, 53, 54, 104, 105, 108; and US-USSR relations, 50, 67, 104, 106; and unification of Europe, 22, 102; and war danger, 76, 84, 86, 107-108; as world power, xxvi, 72, 106
Free, Lloyd A., xvii, xxviii, 68

111

About the Author

LLOYD A. FREE is the president of the Institute for International Social Research, which to date has polled one-third of the world's population. Earlier, he was a lecturer at Princeton University, associate director of the Princeton Public Opinion Project, and editor of *Public Opinion Quarterly*. Subsequently, he served as senior counselor in charge of mass communications at UNESCO and later directed the State Department's worldwide information program. He has been an advisor to Presidents Eisenhower, Kennedy, and Johnson.